We were there at the BGHSNAA 2024 Reunion!

Amidst the frolic and fun, we reminisced - with our former classmates, colleagues, and mentors - our BGHSN glorious past that ushered our future blissful blessings.

The Why of the ReminiscenceS

No aftermath summary book was published after any Baguio General Hospital School of Nursing (BGHSN) grand international reunions since the First BGHSN International Grand Reunion in July 17-19, 1992, held at Oak Brook Marriott in Illinois, USA. While all the past reunions had so called souvenir program books that had greetings and praises to the organizers, advertisements to finance the printing cost of the books, and program of what would happen during the reunion, NOTHING could and would be devoted to what really happened during the reunion itself.

That 'NOTHING' comprises what happened during the reunion. That 'NOTHING' is the total experience of what had transpired – the re-bonding camaraderie, the fun, the excitement – among those who attended the reunion. That 'Nothing' should have reflected what truly happened during the festivities. This makes so called 'souvenir programs' a misnomer. This makes the 'NOTHING' the real souvenir of the smiles, the hugs, the dances, ringing laughter, music, and more – but alas could be lost in memory for there are no general records of the 'Nothing.'

True, individuals could have their own records in individual pictures or videos they have taken but those moments would only remain among themselves who could treasure them. However, all shares the general gatherings, and everyone should have a treasury of all the moments shared by everyone.

Done, but the memories of merriment, ringing music, banters, and bonding will forever remain and linger.

The ReminiscenceS

This is where the ReminiscenceS of the 12th Baguio General Hospital School of Nursing Alumni Association (BHGHSNAA) International Grand Reunion comes to fore.

For the first time since the BGHSNAA's past reunions, ReminiscenceS tries to recapture the grand exuberance generated during the reunion of Oct. 11-13, 2024, to ring out for the future years as one flips through the pages of the Book. Those who were at the reunion will have a collective memory on how we danced; how we modeled our dresses, how we broke out into guffaws as we recalled hilarious snippets of our past; how we shared our successful professional journey stories; how we bonded with our former classmates, schoolmates, mentors, and administrators; and most of all how we expressed our gratitude to the institution that paved our niches in serving society as professional medical providers.

Yes, what happened in San Diego in Oct. 11-13, 2024, cannot just stay in San Diego. It will ring forever in the pages of ReminiscenceS – and designed to last.

The ReminiscenceS Staff | *Content Coordinator* - **Fona Fornasdoro**, *Content Contributor* - **Nida Cristobal**, *Layout and Photography* - **Rudy D. Liporada**, *Photography* - **Roy 'Saleng Ken Marapait' Reclosado**, *Video Contributor* - **Bert Magsino**

BGHSNAA-Southern California

Thank You for the Jubilation!

The recent Alumni reunion at the Marriott Marquis was more than just an event; it was a jubilation of lifelong connections. Every photograph captured the essence of joy as friends, acquaintances, and new friends created lasting memories together. These moments are invaluable, surpassing the worth of any high-end material possessions that often gather dust in our closets. They don't just reside in our memories but also in our hearts, leaving a lasting impact that we will cherish forever.

Whenever we recall these experiences, we can't help but smile as they transport us back to those magical moments. This reunion has carved a permanent place in our memories that we will carry with us. Thank you, BGHSNAASC, for gifting us these extraordinary memories that will last a lifetime.

Bienvenida Cristobal, Class '69

ReminisenceS

The ReminiscenceS Staff

Bert Magsino
Video Support

Bienvenida Cristobal
Class '69
Reunion Book
Committee Member
Content Contributor

Fona Fornasdoro
Class '77,
with Ed Fornasdoro,
Reunion Book
Committee Chair
Content Coordinator

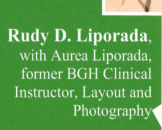

Rudy D. Liporada,
with Aurea Liporada,
former BGH Clinical
Instructor, Layout and
Photography

Roy 'Saleng Ken Marapait' Reclosado,
with Irma Molina Ferrer,
Class '76,
Photography

We love to capture, gather, and preserve telling moments to speak for eternity.

Anyone who is included in this publication and would like their pictures or comments deleted, please speak out before the publication of Reminiscences so we could remove said items from The book before ReminiscenceS is published. Otherwise, all materials herein are considered permitted for publication.

November 03, 2024

The comments on the BGHSNAA site clearly express a common sentiment: we have created lasting memories together. The recent event provided a wonderful opportunity to reconnect and reflect on our shared experiences.

A heartfelt thank you to all the Alumni and guests who participated and helped make this celebration so meaningful. Your involvement truly enriched the occasion!

Happy Thanksgiving, everyone!
BGHSNAA-SC Officers & members

BGHSNAASC
12th BGHSNAA INTERNATIONAL GRAND REUNION
Marriott Marquis San Diego Marina
333 West Harbor Dr., San Diego, CA 92101
Date: October 11, 12, 13, 2024

Good evening, everyone!

My name is Crisabel Ramos, Over-All-Chair of the Planning Committee for our 12th BGHSNAA Grand International Reunion. It was a privilege welcoming our distinguished Guest Speaker, Ms. Marieta Gaddi, fellow alumni, beloved guests and friends.

As President of BGHSNAASC, I was deeply honored to acknowledge the collective efforts that made our Grand Reunion a triumph! I salute the Planning Committee, alumni, donors and sponsors for their remarkable contributions that are truly immeasurable. Your unwavering commitment, generosity, and camaraderie have forged lasting bonds.

On behalf of BGHSNAA SOUTHERN CALIFORNIA, we are delighted to have you all joined us in this magnificent celebration of our 12th Grand Reunion. May the 3-day Celebration have brought nostalgia and magical moments for a lifetime memory. I do appreciate many of you that travelled long distances which reminded us on how we valued the comradeship brought to us by our nursing school leaders, mentors and well-seasoned clinical instructors that led us to how we became professionals today. Thank you so much for your wonderful support!

This year our theme is "Living the BGHSN Legacy!" Yes, we are living witnesses to how we have struggled the nursing student life, overcame challenges, and bridged the gap of all class years and gathered us altogether as alumni in every school reunion. Our alumni organization is all what we have. We can forever value our reunions, treasuring and enjoying the nostalgia shared between us. Our keynote speaker inspired us with wealth of wisdom; the sumptuous food filled our hunger pangs; the marvelous cultural dancers sparked the room full of energy and happiness! Our special comedian from Hollywood, Rob Schneider, thrilled us with full of excitement! I am sure that your hearts jumped with joy and delight with the incredible gift prizes.

Our magnificent emcees, Ms. Connie Asiong, Class '69, and Mr. Robert Villa, Class '71, surely engaged with us, making sure that we were all entertained. What a stellar performance!

Fellow alumni, guests and friends, this phenomenal grand reunion brought us a spectacular, memorable experience, indeed! The Welcome Night and Gala Night were two nights worth remembering to include the magnificent picnic on the third day with so much cultural favorite dishes!

I want to express once more my warm gratitude on behalf of the BGHSNAASC Steering Committee, officers, and members of the Planning Committee for your unwavering love and exceptional loyalty and devotion to our beloved Alma Mater through BGHSNAA with your physical presence! We could not have done this without you! We were all beyond amazed with the turn out. Certainly, it was an immense pleasure seeing many of you here in San Diego! MABUHAY!!

Crisabel Ramos, RN
BGHSNAASC President
2023-22025

A Trajectory towards the Reunion's Success

On behalf of the ReminiscenceS staff, I would like to express our thanks to the Southern California (SC) Planners and Organizers for permitting us to serve the BGHSNAA in terms of our efforts to journal the successful 12th international reunion event. We had promised to capture, gather snippets, and preserve the telling moments of the tremendously successful event. Tremendous is, to us, an understatement. The joyous emotions exuded during the reunion's three-day event is far beyond measure.

Albeit, we hope that, with The Aftermath, we fulfilled our promise of providing you with a treasure book chest of memories of the event.

Nonetheless, an important vignette of the success of the event that we could not capture but worthy of preserving is the trajectory that culminated in the Oct. 11-13, 2024, reunion success. Not to mention this trajectory is watering down what could have been the success of earlier organizers of what should have been. The story of the recent event would also not be complete.

Thus…

Proud of holding past four successful reunions of BGHSNAA, the Southern California (SC) group of the Association vied and won again to hold the 12th international reunion right after the 11th held in Baguio City in February 2019.

Shortly after coming back to the mainland from the Philippines, picking up from initial talks while still at Camp John Hay in Baguio City, the SC officers and members immediately established the committees that would place the 12th underway. They initiated meetings and set June 25-27, 2021, as the reunion date. They identified the Queen Mary, once a ship for the affluent and turned into a warship, now docked at Long Beach as a premier hotel, for the venue. Deciding with the place, they reserved it with a hefty deposit.

Alas! COVID-19 struck.

With everything at a standstill and with no clear future in sight, everything was dropped, including losing the deposit made for the Queen Mary. With all the uncertainties, everyone wondered if a 12th reunion would still be held.

Then the COVID-19 air slowly came to pass.

Among other things coming to light, queries came, at first, in trickles, then in frenzy. Are we still holding the 12th? Will we resume meetings? When and where are we holding it?

Within that time, the BGHSNAA-SC transitioned under a new presidency in 2022. Picking up from the past administration's accomplishments, meetings resumed with the bulk of the pre-COVID committee members serving in the continuum. The new set dates were for October 11-13, 2024, at the Marriott Marquis in San Diego, California.

We can say that the success of the 12th International Reunion was a trajectory from a pent-up wanting to hold one with COVID hovering as a factor against it being held; and a successful overcoming it with the determination of members - combining the expertise of the veterans and enthusiasm of the new members - of the BGHSNAA-SC to hold it.

For this, we congratulate the planners and organizers of the recent held San Diego reunion for their unwavering efforts for its formidable success. We would also like to thank all those supporting the ReminiscenceS as it progressed to fruition. They were the inspiration for having it and we, of the staff, are so happy that we have fulfilled our goal of providing a most wholesome, to reiterate, treasure book of memories of the event.

More power to the BGHSNAA and the BGHSNAA-SC

We hope to be there when you do it again.

On behalf of Nida Cristobal, Ed and Fona Fornasdoro, Saleng Ken Marapait, and Bert Magsino,

I remain,

Rudy D. Liporada

What we were, are, and will be

My Fellow Alumni,

It is a privilege and pleasure to be with you tonight.

Some of us have traveled far and wide to celebrate this momentous event, anticipating to create beautiful memories and precious moments to last us a lifetime.

We are proud to be alumni of our beloved Baguio General Hospital School of Nursing.

I belong to class 1961, 63 years ago, proud and honored to be a product of a prestigious school.

What we are today is a product of many factors, conditions, situations, choices, and responses but mostly the influence of a solid foundation of education with competence and compassion we earned at BGHSN.

We are the professional nurses who are BGHSN's contribution to the nursing profession and to the world.

The theme of my message involves the three stages of our professional life, which are:

What we were - Our Past
What we are - Our Present
What we will be - Our Future

What we were

We started nursing as workers, where we always gave our best wherever we worked, whatever was expected of us.

We started eight hours work in addition to academics. Thus, twelve hours of duty was not new to us.

We gave our best in the clinical area in the community, in the classrooms as managers and practitioners.

We manifested excellent skills and competence coupled with dedication and commitment.

We excelled in whatever field of endeavors we were engaged in and gained personal satisfaction, good relationships, hefty monetary remunerations for some, and for everyone - self-actualization and realization of self-worth.

This is the physical aspect of the professional.

What we are

The second role as professionals that involves the mind is - What are we today.

Through our work, we have given the young generations role models of service which we hope they can emulate.

The young professionals, our children are affected by what we do, are living witnesses to the fulfillment we have in doing what we are expected of us to do.

They chose the nursing profession. They chose to be like us in terms of skills and competence.

Believe me, our influence is felt everyday, everywhere. We influence their minds.

What we will be

Our third role is - What we will be in spirit.

Our presence is needed in order to influence but, when we inspire, we do it even in our absence, for whatever the new generation does today is thought about by their own aspiration and motivation.

That actions of the younger generations are their own validation, to be the best of whatever they are to be competent, to be dedicated and committed to their calling.

Not every professional is able to inspire, not everyone's influence is felt. and not all persons give their best all the time.

I am proud to say that we, the BGHSN alumni did give our best.

We were competent, dedicated, and committed to the nursing profession.

We have influenced many young generations to continue what we have began, serving as role models, and we served as inspirations for the profession to move onward and forward, giving the best care to the world.

Thank you for the opportunity to serve in our past with our body, to influence with our minds today, and to inspire in the future.

Let's continue our journey, leave a legacy in the minds and spirits of our colleagues.

More Power to the BGHSN Alumni!
More Power to the Nursing Profession!

Marieta Herrera-Gaddi
Class '61

12th Baguio General Hospital School of Nursing Alumni Association International Reunion

Planners and Organizers

Seated (l-r) Mary Abiaro, Aurora Baduria, Connie Asiong, Mildred Hizon, Nellie dela Peña, Mila Seguban, Tess Gaetos, Carrie Ramos, Crisabel Ramos, Merle Arceo

Standing (l-r) Arsenia Smith, Robert Villa, Art De Vera, Josie Mejia, Thelma Velbis, Zeny Bersamira, Fona Fornasdoro, Naty Savellno, Aurora Manrique, Tess Vidal, Herman Mallare, Wilfred Ballesil

Not in Picture: Zeny Razalan, Evilia Liganor, Nida Cristobal, Josie Ruiz, Lorna Baird, Brenda Leal, Myrna Aganos, Gloria Duty

- Great job! No regrets coming! - Rolly
- Thanks for the officers who organized this reunion. Am so happy to attend from Baguio - Purificacion
- Thanks for the great memories BGHSNAA! - Gloria
- I can't thank you enough for your effort for this reunion. - Rachel
- Stories are endless After so many decades …. we have more pleasantries to share – Gina
- Thank You all for organizing a great Grand Reunion - lifetime memories to cherish - Tess
- It was such a wonderful, memorable experience - Marivic
- Thank you Ading Cris or your great works and all of you who helped made our event so wonderful and memorable one. - Aurelia
- Thank you for the privilege being part of a momentous event! Well organized and well managed! - Marietta
- Thank you event committee. It was a wonderful party - Joy

12th BGHSNAA INTERNATIONAL GRAND REUNION
October 11-13, 2024

THANK YOU, ALUMNI & FRIENDS!

BGHSNAA-SC officers & members

Baguio General Hospital School of Nursing
Alumni Association of Southern California
Officers 2023-2025

Crisabel Ramos
President

Thelma Velbis
Vice-President

Mary Abiaro
Recording Secc.

Officers

Crisabel Tabeta Ramos, Class '74
President

Thelma Mayo Velbis, Class '70
Vice-President

Mary Asiong Abiaro, Class '77
Recording Secretary

Aurora Regacho Baduria, Class '71
Treasurer

Zeny de Guzman Razalan, Class '69
Assistant Treasurer

Evilia Martin Liganor, Class '59
Auditor

Arsenia Zeny Smith, Class '77
Connie S. Asiong, Class '69
Press Relations Officers

Josie Mayo Ruiz, Class '68
Lorna Baird, Class '68
Zenaida Flores Bersamira, Class '69
Fona Fornasdoro, Class '77
Representatives – San Diego

Aurora Baduria
Treasurer

Zeny Razalan
Asst. Treasurer

Evilia Martin-Liganor
Auditor

Arsenia Smith
PRO

Connie Asiong
PRO

Josie Ruiz
Rep-San Diego

Lorna Baird
Rep-San Diego

Zeny Bersamira
Rep-San Diego

Fona Fornasdoro
Rep-San Diego

Mildred Hizon
Rep-Los Angeles

Nellie dela Pena
Rep-Los Angeles

Brenda Leal
Rep-Los Angeles

Josie Mejia
Rep-Los Angeles

Merle Arceo
Rep-San Bernadino

Myrna Aganos
Rep-San Bernardino

Officers

Mildred Hizon, Class '65
Nellie dela Pena, Class '65
Brenda Leal, Class '70
Josie Raquedan Mejia, Class '74
Representatives - Los Angeles

Merle Arceo, Class '77
Myrna Aganos, Class '77
Representatives-San Bernardino

Robert Villa, Class '71
Herman Mallare, Class '71
Arturo DeVera, Class '71
Wilfred Ballesil, Class '71
Logistics

Carrie Buyao Ramos, Class '61
Tess Gaetos, Class '61
Mila Ferriols Seguban, Class '62
Advisors

Gloria Espiritu Duty, Class '57
Honorary Advisor

Robert Villa
Logistics

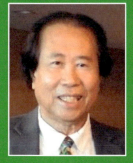
Herman Mallare
Logistic

Arthur DeVera
Logistics

Wilfred Ballesil
Logistics

Carrie Ramos
Advisor

Tess Gaetos
Advisor

Mila Seguban
Advisor

Gloria Duty
Honorary Advisor

Baguio General Hospital School of Nursing
Alumni Association of Southern California
12ᵗʰ International Grand Reunion

Marriott Marquis, San Diego Marina - October 11-13, 2024

Committees

Steering
Chairperson: *Crisabel Ramos*
Members: *Carrie Ramos, Nida S. Cristobal, Tess Gaetos, Connie S. Asiong*

Sign-in & Welcome
Chair: *Aurora Baduria*
Co-Chair: *Zeny Razalan*
Members: *Mary Abiaro, Zeny Bersamira, Josie Ruiz, Eva Rodrigo Mamaril, Josie Mejia, Naty Rimorin Savellano, Merle Arceo, Fona Fornasdoro, Irma Molina, Aurora Manrique, Cristina Lao, Thelma Velbis*

Reception & Seating
Chair: *Nellie dela Peña*
Co-Chair: *Mildred Hizon*
Members: *Mila Segoban, Julita Cabillan, Conni Tess Reyes Vidal, Bumanglag Alcon, Teresita Reyes Vidal, Jovet Jose*

Logistics
Chair: *Herman Mallare*
Co-Chair: *Robert Villa*
Members: *Art De Vera, Wilfred Ballesil*

Decoration
Chair: *Mel Madrid*
Co-Chair: *Josie Ruiz*
Members: *Arsenia 'Zeny' Smith, Elvira Bautista, Nellie Bumanglag Arcon, Lorna Baird, Crisabel Ramos*

Program
Chair: *Connie Salaza Asiong*
Co-Chair: *Crisabel Ramos*
Members: *Carrie Ramos, Tess Gaetos, Nida Cristobal, Thelma Velbis, Robert Villa*

Reunion Book & Advertisement
Chair: *Fona Fornasdoro*
Co-Chair: *Crisabel Ramos*
Members: *Nida S. Cristobal, Josie Ruiz, Thelma Velbis, Rudy D. Liporada, Zenaida Razalan, Aurora Baduria*

Picnic
Chair: *Thelma Velbis*
Co-Chair: *Herman Mallare*
Members: *Logistics, All BGHSNAASC, Officers, and Com Members*

Master and Mistress of Ceremonies for Welcome and Gala Nights
Robert Villa
Connie Asiong

Special Donors

We would like to extend our appreciation and gratitude to the following alumni for their resources and efforts donated beyond what had been asked from all attendees that helped made this 12th BGHSNAA International Grand Reunion a success!

Salamat Po!

Connie Salaza Asiong Class '69

Frank and Arsenia Smith Class '77

Herman and Fortune Mallare Class '71

Josefina Soriano Goldin Class '71

Nida S. Cristobal Class '69

Teresita Gaetos Class '61

Art de Vera Class '71

Zeny de Guzman Razalan Class '69

Zeny Flores Bersamira Class '69

Alma A. Vistro Class '69

Lorna Casarino Baird Class '68

Carrie B. Ramos Class '61

Crisabel Tabeta Ramos Class '74

Thelma Mayo Velbis Class '70

Josie Mayo Ruiz Class '68

Virgil and Aurora Baduria Class '71

Eddie and Fona Fornasdoro Class '77

Robert and Pinky Villa Class '71

Mary Asiong Abiaro Class '77

Merle E. Arceo Class '77

Natividad Rimorin Savellano Class '76

Aurora Boado Manrique Class '76

Myrna Estigoy Aganos Class '77

Special Acknowledgement
To Our Planning Hosts

Merle Espiritu Arceo
Class 1977 - Clairemont, CA

Art de Vera & Rheza Antonio
Class 1971 - Diamond Bar, CA

Jesusa Pascua Macayan
Class 1958 - Huntington Beach, CA

Herman & Fortune Mallare
Class 1971 - Escondido, CA

Art and Melecia Edra - Madrid
Class 1967 - Wildomar, CA

Fred (+) & Carrie Buyao - Ramos
Class 1961 - Buena Park, CA

Lee & Zenaida de Guzman - Razalan
Class 1969 - Rancho Palos Verdes, CA

Frank & Arsenia Gonzales - Smith
Class 1977 - Vista, CA

Romeo & Tess Reyes -Vidal
Class 1979 - Chino Hills, CA

Planning for the 12th BGHSNAA International Grand Reunion actually started in 2019 and was slated for June of 2021 (See article on The Reunion That Never Was). Unfortunately, the COVID pandemic hit and all the plans went awry with no visions of what the future held. Nonetheless, right after the CDC mandated that masks were no longer necessary and vaccination came to fore as signs that the pandemic was controlled, the planning committee gathered again - in earnest as early as the initial months of 2022. Most weekends were not spared to iron out the fruition of this October 11-13 event. All throughout the months of preparations, the above individuals and families opened their residences to host the meetings. Amidst party like atmosphere, the planners evolved the reunion celebration this weekend. We acknowledge and thank them for their generosity.

Voices from the Past

Their messages were delivered for specific graduating classes for those specific times. However, their words ring for all graduates of the BGHSN and true for all times - they remind us of who we are, still in practice or retired - nurses whose journey to service and success in life root from what we learned from the Baguio General Hospital School of Nursing. We pay tribute to our guiding mentors for their shaping us into who we are.

Republic of the Philippines
BAGUIO GENERAL HOSPITAL AND MEDICAL CENTER
Baguio City

MESSAGE

Welcome Home.

We are very happy to have you back where you belong. Home are the nurses, from over the sea. Home are the Nightingales to beloved BGH School of Nursing. Back to old familiar places. Back to old familiar faces. The old place has changed. Many of the old friends and colleagues are gone or are going. Let us enjoy each other's company while it lasts. The time will come when there will be no more alumni to remember the sweet old times at BGHSN. The great school that BGHSN was and the many noble graduates it has produced will simply pass into history. We are her legacy.

AURORA PE BENITO TENEFRANCIA
Class of 1955

Message

Congratulations to all the members of Class '69 and especially to your parents and guardians.

I shall share with your happiness on this memorable occasion. I hope that the future will give the Baguio General Hospital School of Nursing even more reason to be happy and proud of you. For what greater reward we can ask for than to know that our graduates are doing well wherever they may be.

This is my wish . . . this is my prayer on this Graduation Day.

Sgd. (Mrs.) CLOTILDA L. TOM
Principal & Officer-in-charge, Nursing Service

Republic of the Philippines
Ministry of Health-Region I
DR. EFRAIN C. MONTEMAYOR MEDICAL CENTER
(BAGUIO GENERAL HOSPITAL AND MEDICAL CENTER)
Baguio City

MESSAGE

This is another happy milestone in your lives which I would like to share with your loved ones. Treasure whatever you have learned from your instructors, their advice, and even their scoldings for all these things will bring you to greater heights in the practice of your Chosen Career. Be proud of your Alma Mater and uphold its name by doing what is good and true.

To the Members of the Graduating Class of 1984, my heartfelt congratulations.

ARACELI P. PIONG, RN, BSN, NA
Chief Nurse IV

The Painting at the Lobby

To a BGHSN Alumni

Surely, as a former nursing student, you would have passed by the Amorsolo painting depicting Jesus Christ over humanity through the main corridor of the Baguio General Hospital. Surely, you have not missed noticing that there is a nurse among the mass of humanity in the painting. The painting's title is 'Our Blessed Lord and Some of His Children.'

In your rush to go to your stations to do whatever you had to do, you may just have glanced at it; over time, you were aware of it, but not conscious of why it was there.

The nurse in the painting depicts YOU, a student evolving to become a nurse. Through the power of sublimation, you were unconsciously being imbued with the morals and values of your niche in society – that of providing the tender loving care to anyone who might need aid as patients, guided by the principles of love as taught by Jesus Christ.

Yes, your love to serve is paramount over all the skills and knowledge you have acquired from the Baguio General Hospital School of Nursing.

You serve or have served well, guided by Christlike value and morals – and are endowed, in return, with immense blessings for you and your family.

Humanity thanks you for your service.

The Amorsolo Painting

In the late 1940s, it is said that BGH Dr. Ireneo Geslani treated George Barterr, a British Anglican missionary. The doctor did not accept any fee for his service. In return, the missionary commissioned Fernando Amorsolo to do the painting for $450.00. It took the renowned Filipino artist three years to complete the painting. The missionary donated the painting through his personal physician to the Baguio General Hospital in 1952. The painting is now worth, at least, P20M.

While the hospital was undergoing renovations, the painting was stolen on May 21, 1998. Forty-one days later, art collector Manuel Morato bought it for P1.5M. He would later realize that it was stolen because, in his estimate, it could have fetched P14M. He then made efforts to know where it came from. Learning that it was from BGH, he decided to donate it back after he had it restored.

The painting needed to be restored because it was folded and not rolled, causing it to have creases. The restoration took two years.

It was unveiled and back at the hospital's lobby since April 13, 2000.

Oh! Yes. We were there!

Attendees

Names: Last, First, Middle		Class
Cabula, Rosita	Serdenia	56
Duty, Gloria	Espiritu	57
Macayan, Jesusa	Pascua	58
Liganor, Evilia	Martin	59
Botuyan, Irene Deana	Furagganan	61
Da Veiga, Bibiana	Hidalgo	61
Fangonil, Anita	Della Herrera	61
Gaddi, Marietta		61
Gaetos, Teresita		61
Ramos, Carrie	Buyao	61
Zuraek, Adelaida	Haban	61
Bulacan, Arsenia	Duldulao	62
Dazo, Luz	Perena	62
Nerona, Estrellita	Padilla	62
Salcedo, Severina	Alvendia	62
Seguban, Mila	Ferriols	62
Calica, Warnito		63
Rios, Eunice	Bilagot	63
Valerio, Manuel	R	63
Ranchez, Prudencio		64
dela Pena, Cornelia (Nellie)	Arquero	65
Hizon, Mildred	Cortes	65
Alaan, Dolores	San Pedro	66
Fitzsimmons, Jeanie	Molina	66
Gutierrez, Edna	Rivera	66
Balisi, Olivia	Bernardez	66
Ramiro, Teresita	Eugenio	66
Rodrigo, Teresita	Obrar	66
Aguam, Zenaida	Canilao	67
Bayani, Delia	Leung	67
Fontanilla, Wilfreda	Corpuz	67
Madrid, Melecia	Edra	67
Mendoza, Edelia	De Venecia	67
Pimentel, Evelyn	Ancheta	67
Santos, Crispina	Colcol	67
Torio, Fe	Bermio	67
Torres, Cecilia	Herrera	67
Villamil, Evangeline	Mejia	67
Baird, Lorna	Casarino	68
Lopez, Marylyn	Asprer	68
Ruiz, Josephine	Mayo	68
Sali, Jane	Tano	68
Spiro, Lolita	Flores	68
Tabora, Nerisa	Lagatao	68
Angeles, Rebecca	Ramos	69
Arnoldi, Eva	Manlongat	69
Asiong, Connie	Salaza	69
Bayle, Eleanor	Daclan	69
Bersamin, Eufemia	Ducusin	69
Bersamira, Zenaida	Flores	69
Cabugao, Jane	Cawis	69
Cristobal, Bienvenida	Sotto	69
Largo, Milagros	Rimando	69
Luna, Jocelyn	Orden	69
Olais, Beatrice	V.	69
Razalan, Zenaida	de Guzman	69
Santillan, Beatriz	Espinoza	69
Vistro, Alma	Abellera	69
Alagar, Gracia	Burdeos	70
Castro, Amelia	Cabreros	70
Davis, Zinnia	Cacdac	70
Dimdiman, Estrelita	Gonzales	70
Duguid, Nelia	Carpiso	70
Dy, Mary	Paynor	70
Felmley, Alma	Dizon	70
Go, Remedios	Rivera	70
Leal, Brenda	R.	70
Madayag, Tomas	C.	70
Martinez, Procisimo	M.	70
McGee, Dolly	Bautista	70
Molina, Arlene	Austria	70
Panaga, Luz	Valdez	70
Quiros, Remedios	Directo	70
Rivera, Helen	Beltran	70
Sanchez, Angelita	Lorezco	70
Soriano, Grace	Vergara	70
Tagupa, Grace	C	70
Velbis, Thelma	Mayo	70
Villanueva, Veronic	Adriano	70
Wood, Florentina	Serquina	70
Baduria, Aurora	Regacho	71
Ballesil, Wilfred	D.	71
de Vera, Art	T.	71
Doria, Alicia	Delacruz	71
Fernandez, Mae	Baltazar	71
Guevarra, Corazon	Laranang	71

Attendees

Names: Last, First, Middle		Class
Gutierrez, Corazon	Tejada	71
Mallare, Herman	R.	71
Manuel, Cecilia	Tolentino	71
Moll, Susana	Valdez	71
Quijano, MayRose	Paynor	71
Villa, Robert	C.	71
Dizon, Cory	Consenco	72
Udasco Jr, Ismael	Navarro	72
Abalos, Ramona	Nicolas	73
Ancheta, Lillian	Lachica	73
Carbonell, Cathy	Cacananta	73
Chua, Divinia	Barcelo	73
Estepa, Avelina	Dulay	73
Francisco, Rebecca	Ramos	73
Gonzales, Josefina	Madrid	73
Joaquin, Primrose	De Leon	73
Laberinto, Adoracion	Selga	73
Ligeralde, Fe	Antonio	73
Mangalino, Aurelia	Medrano	73
Quinto, Violeta	Casillan	73
Ramirez, Ruel	C.	73
Reyes, Nelly	Dawana	73
Alcon, Nellie	Bumanglag	74
Bambico, Perla	Orin	74
Baterina, Teresita	Marrero	74
Bautista, Virginia	Ramos	74
Belmonte, Rosario	Laranang	74
Bulayo, Esther	Copero	74
Cabillan, Julieta	Leal	74
Cabrera, Yolanda	Gonzalo	74
Danggol, Myrna	Calatan	74
Domingo, Carmelita	Ramos	74
Edrozo, Cory	Francisco	74
Javier, Marissa	Roaquin	74
Macaraeg, Carolina	David	74
Mamaril, Eva	Rodrigo	74
Marinas, Myrna	Belmonte	74
Mejia, Josie	Raquedan	74
Navaid, Lumen	Reyes	74
Nilo, Whelma	Sales	74
Noe, Jocelyn	Basilio	74
O'Mary, Elena	Cruz	74
Pinera, Emiliana Tabora	Colis	74
Nerisa	Ramos	74
Platt, Elizabeth	Hamada	74
Ramos, Crisabel	Tabeta	74
Salazar, Elsa	Serrano	74
Sarmiento, RubyAnn,	Pobre	74
Sison, Maria Luisa	Garcia	74
Bullecer, Jane	Chinsio	75
Frigillana, Rachel	G.	75
Guideng, Joy	Lagman	75
Gumayagay, Vicky	Ventura	75
Abalos, Josephine	Espino	76
Adviento, Edna Belen	Rodriguez	76
Alonso, Erminda	Torralba	76
Calpito, Caroline	Gomez	76
Castro, Susan	Guzman	76
Congjuico, Judith		76
Corpuz, Lilian	Calamiong	76
Espejo, Jocelyn	Almonte	76
Ferrer, Irma	Molina	76
Garcia, Myrna	Talento	76
Guerrero, Divina	Ramos	76
Gumabon, Leonarda	Guillermo	76
Jose, Jovet	Flores	76
Lao, Cristina	Yapyap	76
Lewkowics, Dinah	Imbat	76
Lumanlan, Arlene	Cantre	76
Manrique, Aurora	Boado	76
Pacalso, Jane	Galpo	76
Peralta, Teresita	L.	76
Postadan, Carmelita	Cave	76
Radam, Flordeliza	Cabatic	76
Savellano, Maria Natividad	Rimorin	76
Tabajonda, Zenaida	Javier	76
Tamayo, Brenda	Calimlim	76
Abiaro, Mary	Asiong	77
Aganos, Myrna	Estigoy	77
Arceo, Merle	Espiritu	77
Ayeo, Helen	Aoay	77
Bassig, Erlinda	B.	77
Bautista, Elvira	Gonatice	77
Carlos, Elenita	Timbuloy	77
Darrow, Celia	Cabigas	77
Fine, Henry		77
Fornasdoro, Trifona	Raguro	77

Attendees

Names: Last, First, Middle	Class
Gayomba, Arsenia Ramos	77
Guanzon, Norma Tadina	77
Imus, Julita Untalan	77
Lardizabal, Lyne Rivera	77
Magalued, Concepcion Egmin	77
Martinez, Virginia Esperon	77
Pulicay, Juliet Abalos	77
Smith, Arsenia Gonzales	77
Strutner, Eden Jaravata	77
Villa, Henry P.	77
Bassig, Loreta dela Cruz	78
Calimlim, Ludivica S.	78
Evangelista, Evelyn Gonzalo	78
Gapasin, Carol Manuel	78
Gonzales, Evelyn Obay	78
Tigno, Florence Bigornia	78
Villa, Nancy Manuel	78
Alimurung, Thelma Limos	79
Angeles, Lilia dela Vega	79
Aquino, Jocelyn Ayson	79
Asuncion, Dolores	79
Azarcon, Avito	79
Batan, Marlyn Abando	79
Bautista, Myrna Vitales	79
Beronia, Leonora Esperanza	79
Blount, Wilma Emily Bonsato	79
Boontiang, Myrna Balinbin	79
Caballar, Gloria Ditas Foronda	79
Aquino, Georgina Cadalin	79
Calamiong, Rudy	79
Camero, Helen Cabrito	79
Canubas, Elena Daplian	79
Casem, Carolino "Roland"	79
Castaneto, Nicetas Geslani	79
Cho, Cecilia Hulog	79
Clifford, Gloria	79
Corpuz, Vivien Ballucanag	79
Cuison, Teresita Lorezco	79
De Vera, Marlene Soliven	79
El-Sahn, Bing Barberan	79
Espiritu, Carolyn Espino	79
Gaengan, Juliet Gawe	79
Galo, Jane Cambod	79
Guillermo, Veronica T.	79
Gumpeng, Virginia Tanacio	79
Hoffman, Susan Calica	79
La Madrid, Marco	79
Llorente, Myrna Estrada	79
Lomibao, Mary Ann Ocsan	79
Mabutas, Leonora Cerezo	79
Macaraeg, Percy Soriano	79
Macatol, Loida Ancheta	79
Manangan, Merlita Manuel	79
Mananquil, Milagros Tiongson	79
Nalundasan, Nivas Lyn Bautista	79
Padcayan, Paula Socnayan	79
Paras, Blanquita Dalaten	79
Pedro, Lydia Abuan	79
Perez, Candy Quisquisan	79
Pinera, Shirley	79
Quero, Evangeline Mangaliag	79
Quidangen, Benjie	79
Rabot, Ricardo A.	79
Ragudos, Abraham	79
Reyes, Reynaldo	79
Saclolo, Bernadette Manzano	79
Sadcopen, Agustina Siblagan	79
Salanga, Rosalia Chanpay	79
Salvatoriello, Nora Cuison	79
Sanchez, Rosemarie Sahoy	79
Santos, Eva Aquino	79
Songcuan, Vida Balbin	79
Sural, Connie Manalo	79
Tigno, Romeo	79
Torres, Mary Jane	79
Trinidad, Florencia Ganir	79
Caloncagon, Marlyn Ubaldo	79
Vidal, Theresa Reyes	79
Villa, Josephine Pelias	79
Welch, Marites Espejo	79
Busacay, Noemi Soberano	81
Falatico, Marivic Guidangen	82
Figueros, Marieta Corpuz	82
Padernal, Esther Jalandoni	82
Estigoy, Roland G.	83

12th BGHSNAA Grand International Reunion Attendance

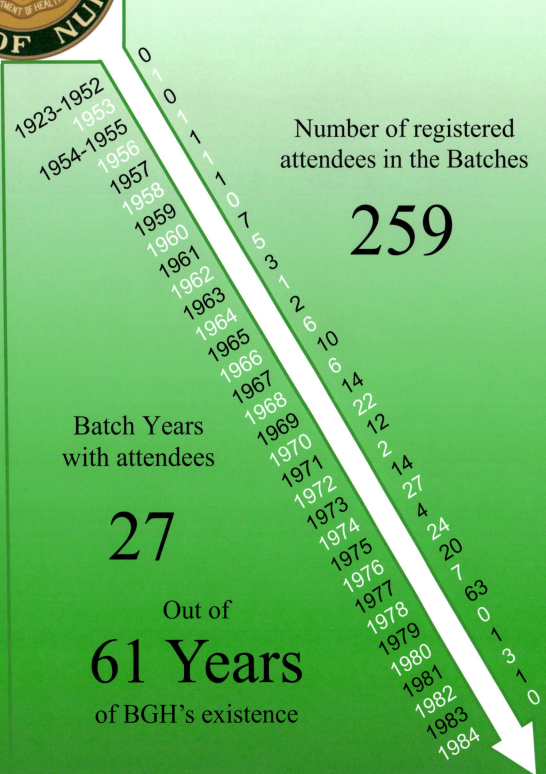

Number of registered attendees in the Batches

259

Batch Years with attendees

27

Out of

61 Years

of BGH's existence

Batch Year	Attendees
1923-1952	0
1953	1
1954-1955	0
1956	1
1957	1
1958	1
1959	0
1960	7
1961	5
1962	3
1963	1
1964	2
1965	6
1966	10
1967	6
1968	14
1969	22
1970	12
1971	2
1972	14
1973	27
1974	4
1975	24
1976	20
1977	7
1978	63
1979	0
1980	1
1981	3
1982	1
1983	0
1984	

1950s

Crescencia Tamayo Vinluan
Class 1953

Rosita Serdenia-Cabula
Class 1956

Gloria Espiritu-Duty
Class 1957

Jesusa Pascua Macayan
Class 1958

Evilia Martin Liganor
Class 1959

Special Mention Attendee

Marrieta Herrera Gaddi
Class '61
Reunion Guest Speaker

1961
Aida Zuraek, Bing DaVeiga, Tess Gaetos,
Marietta Gaddi, Carrie Ramos, Annie Fangonil

1962
L-R: Mila Ferriols Seguban, Estrelita Padilla Nerona,
Severina Alvendia Salcedo, Luz Perena Dazo,
Arsenia Duldulao Bulacan

Tess Gaetos '61

Annie Fangonil '61

Carrie Ramos '61

Severina Alvendia Salcedo, '62

Arsenia Duldulao Bulacan, '62

Mila Ferriols Seguban, '62

Bing DaVeiga '61

Marietta Gaddi '61

Aida Zuraek '61

Estrelita Padilla Nerona, '62

Luz Perena Dazo, '62

Warnito Calica '63

Eunice Rios Bilagot, '63

Manuel R. Valerio '63.

1963
L-R: Warnito Calica, Eunice Rios Bilagot, Manuel R. Valerio

1964
Prudencio Ranchez

1965
L-R: Mildred Hizon and Nellie dela Peña

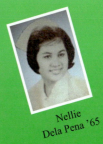
Nellie Dela Pena '65

Mildred Cortes Hizon '65

1966

L-R: Jeannie Molina Fitzsimmons,
Olivia Balisi Bernardez,
Tessie Obrar Rodrigo,
Tessie Eugenio Ramiro,
Edna Rivera Gutierrez,
Dolores Santa Pedro Alaan

Olive Balisi Bernardez, '66

Teresita Obrar Rodrigo, '66

Edna Rivera Gutierrez, '66

Jeannie Molina Fitzsimmons, '66

Dolores San Pedro Alaan, '66

Teresita Eugenio Ramiro, '66

1967

Front, l-r:
Melecia Edra Madrid
Wilfreda Corpuz Fontanilla
Edelia De Venecia Mendoza
Crispina Colcol Santos
Evangeline Mejia Villamil
Back, l-r:
Cecilia Herrera Torres
Fe Bermio Torio
Delia Leung Bayani
Evelyn Ancheta Pimentel
Zenaida Canilao Aguam

Delia Leung Bayani, '67

Zenaida Canilao Aguam, '67

Crispina Colcol Santos, '67

Wilfreda Corpuz Fontanilla, '67

Cecilia Herrera Torres, '67

Evangeline Mejia Villamil, '67

Evelyn Ancheta Pimentel, '67

Edelia De Venecia Mendoza, '67

Melecia Edra Madrid, '67

Fe Bermio Torio, '67

1968

L-R: Lolita Flores-Spiro,
Nerisa Lagatao-Tabora,
Jane Tano-Sali,
Josephine Mayo-Ruiz,
Lorna Casarino-Baird,
Marylyn Asprer-Lopez

Marylyn Asprer Lopez, 68

Josie Ruiz '68

Lolita Spiro '68

Lorna Casarino Baird, '68

Nerisa Lagatao Tabora, '68

Jane Tano Sali, '68

1969

Front:, l-r: Zenaida Flores-Bersamira
Beatriz Espinoza-Santillan,
Rebecca Ramos-Angeles,
Connie Salaza Asiong,
Eleonor Daclan-Bayle,
Eva Manlongat-Arnoldi
Back, l-r: Beatrice Olais
Alma Abellera-Vistro
Zenaida de Guzman-Razalan,
Jane Cawis-Cabugao,
Jocelyn Orden Luna,
Nida S. Cristobal,
Milagros Rimando-Largo,
Eufemia Ducusin-Bersamin

Beatriz Espinosa Santillan, '69

Zenaida de Guzman Razalan, '69

Eufemia Ducusin Bersamin, '69

Alma Abellera Vistro, '69

Rebecca Ramos Angeles, '69

Beatrice N. Olais, '69

Eleanor Daclan Bayle, '69

Zenaida Flores Bersamira '69

Jane Cawis Cabugao, '69

Josephine Orden Luna, '69

Eva Manlongat Arnoldi, '69

Milagros Rimando Largo, '69

Bienvenida Cristobal, '69

Connie Salaza Asiong, 69

Class 1970

Front, l-r: Grace Alagar Burdeos, Tomas Tom Madayag, Helen Beltran Rivera, Luz Valdez Panaga, Grace Vergara Soriano, Zinnia Cacdac Davis, Remedios Rivera Go, Veronic Adriano Villanueva, Amelia Cabreros Castro, Florentino Serquinia Woods, Nelia Carpiso Duguid, Grace Tagupa
Back, l-r: Mary Alma Paynor Dy, Arlene Austria Molina, Thelma Mayo Velbis, Remedios Directo Quiroz, Estela Gonzales Dimdiman, Alma Dizon Felmley, Procisimo Martinez

1971

Front, l-r:
Corazon Tejada-Gutierrez
Aurora Regacho- Baduria
Alicia Delacruz-Doria
Cecilia Tolentino- Manuel
Corazon Laranang-Guevara
Mae Baltazar-Fernandez
Back, l-r:
May Rose Paynor-Quijano
Robert Villa
Herman Mallare
Wilfred Ballesil
Art de Vera
Susana Valdez-Moll

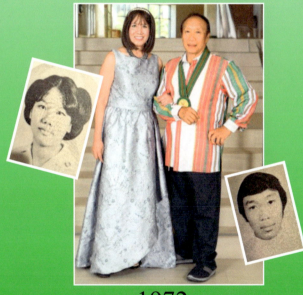

1972
Cory Concenco Dizon
and Ismael Udasco, Jr.

May Rose Paynor Quijano, '71

Herman Mallare '71

Alicia Delacruz Doria '71

Corazon Laranang Guevara, '71

Cecilia Tolentino Manuel, '71

Robert Villa '71

Aurora Regacho Baduria, '71

Art de Vera '71

Corazon Tejada Gutierrez, '71

Susana Valde Moll, '71

Mae Baltaza Fernandez, 71

Wilfred Ballesi '71

1973

Front L-R: Josephine Madrid Gonzales, Dory Selga Laberinto, Divina Barcelo Chua, Nelly Dawana Reyes, Primrose de Leon Joaquin, Avelina Dulay Estepa
Back: L-R: Ramona Nicolas Abalos, Violeta Casillan Quinto, Fe Antonio, Lillian Lachica Ancheta, Aurelia Medrano Magalino, Catalina Cacananta Carbonell, Rebecca Ramos Francisco

Catalina Cacananta Carbonell, '73

Avelina Dulay Estepa, '73

Lillian Lachica Ancheta, '73

Rebecca Ramos Francisco, '73

Nellie Dawana Reyes '73

Primrose de Leon Joaquin, '73

Fe Antonio '73

Josephine Madrid Gonzales, '73

Dory Selga Laberinto, '73

Aurelia Medrano Magalino, '73

Ramona Nicolas Abalos, '73

Divina Barcelo Chua, '73

Violeta Casillan Quinto '73

Golden Jubilarians

 Myrna Calatan Danggol '74
 Marissa Roaquin Javier '74
 Lumen Reyes Navaid '74
 Elizabeth Hamada Platt '74
 Carolina David Macaraeg '74
 Nellie Bumanglag Alcon '74
 Yolanda Gonzalo Cabrera '74
 Corazon Francisco Edrozo, '74

 Eva Rodrigo Mamaril, 74
 Virgie R. Bautista '74
 Emy Pinera '74
 Malou Sison '74
 Jocelyn Noe '74
 Elena O'mary '74
 Julita Leal Cabillan '74
 Crisabel Tabita Ramos '74

 Esther Bulayo '74
 Whelma Sales Nilo '74
 Rose Laranang Belmonte '74
 Teresita Marrero, '74,
 Carmelita Ramos Domingo '74.
 Perla Orin Bambico '74
 Josie Mejia '74
 Elsa Serrano Salazar, '74

1974

Front, l-r:: Carolina David Macaraeg, Yolanda Faustino Cabrera, Perla Orin Bambico, Nellie Bumanglag Alcon, Carmelita Ramos Domingo, Rose Laranang Belmonte, Elena Cruz O'Mary, Esther Copero Bulayo, Elsa Soriano Serrano, Crisabel Tabeta Ramos, Josie Raquedan Mejia, Maria "Malou" Garcia Sison

Back, l-r:: Whelma Sales Nilo, Lumen Reyes Navaid, Virgie Ramos Bautista, Cory Francisco Edrozo, Marissa Roaquin Javier, Teresita Marrero Baterina, Julita Leal Cabillan, Eva Rodrigo Mamaril, Jocelyn Basilio Noe, Elizabeth Hamada Platt, Emi Colis Pinera

1975

L-R : Rachel Gatchalian Frigillana
Jane Chinsio-Bullecer
Victoria Ventura- Gumayagay
Joy Lagman Guideng.

 Arlene Lumanlan '76

 Aurora Boado Manrique, '76

 Divina Ramos Guerrero, '76

 Rachel Gatchalian Frigillana, '75

 Jane Chinsio Bullecer, '75

 Zenaida Javier Tabajonda, '76

 Myrna Talento Garcia, '76

 Erminda Torralba Alonso, '76

 Leonarda G. Gumabon, '76

 Victoria Ventura Gumayagay, '75

 Joy Lagman Guideng, '75

 Purificacion Sahoy Serna, '76

 Susan Guzman Castro, '76

 Lilian Calamiong Corpuz, '76

 Dinah Imbat Lewkowicz, '76

 Jocelyn Espejo '76

Edna Belen R.Adviento '76

 Jane Galpo Pacalso, '76

 Caroline Calpito '76

 Irma Molina Ferrer '76

 Naty Savellano '76

 Teresita Peralta Saludares, '76

 Judith Ponsones Conjuico, '76

 Cristina Yapyap Lao, '76

 Josephine Espino Abalos, '76

 Flordeliza Cabatic Radam, '76

Jovita Flores, '76

1976

Front, l-r: Jocelyn Espejo, Josephine Espino Abalos, Jovet Buenaventura Flores, Judith Ponsones, Flordeliza Cabatic Radam, Divina Guerrero, Natividad Savellano, Susan Guzman, Aurora Boado Manrique, Irma Molina Ferrer, Zenaida Tabajonda
Back, l-r:: Minda Torralba Alonso, Dinah Lewkowicz, Jane Galpo Pacalso, Brenda Tamayo, Carmela Postadan, Edna Belen Rodriguez Adviento, Purification Sahoy, Lilian Calamiong, Teresita Peralta Saludares, Cristina Yapyap Lao, Caroline Calpito

1977

Front, l-r: Henry Fine, Arsenia Gonzalez-Smith, Trifona Raguro- Fornasdoro , Helen Aoay-Ayeo,
Eden Jaravata- Strutner, Celia Cabigas-Darrow, Norma Tadina-Guanzon, Henry Villa
Back, l-r: Myrna Estigoy-Aganos, Arsenia Ramos-Gayomba ,
Erlinda Bassig, Elvira Gonatice-Bautista, Elenita Timbuloy-Carlos, Mary Asiong-Abiaro
Virginia Esperon, Juliet Abalos-Pulicay, Concepcion Egmin-Magalued, Julita Untalan- Imus

Trifona Raguro Fornasdoro '77

Erlinda B. Bassig, '77

Henry Villa '77

Concepcion Magalued '77

Norma Tadina Guanzon, '77

Celia Cabigas Darrow, '77

Arsenia Gonzales Smith, '77

Helen Aoay-Ayeo '77

Eden Jaravata Strutner '77

Arsenia Ramos Gayomba, '77

Juliet Abalos Pulicay, '77

Elenita Timbuloy Carlos, '77

Elvira Gonatice Bautista, '77

Mary Asiong Abiaro '77

Virginia Esperon '77

Julieta Untalan Imus, '77

1978
L-R: Evelyn Gonzalo Evangelista
Loreta de La Cruz Bassig
Evelyn Obay Gonzales
Merle Arceo Alberto
Carol Manuel Gapasin
Nancy Manuel Villa
Ludivica Calimlim
Florence Bigornia Tigno

Nancy Manuel Villa '78

Ludivica Calimlim, 78

Evelyn Obay Gonzales, '78

Carol Manuel Gapasin, '78

Loreta de La Cruz Bassig '78

Evelyn Gonzalo Evangelista, '78

Merle Arceo Alberto, '78

Florence B. Tigno, '78

1979 - 1

Front, l-r: Myrna Labonete Boontiang, Marites Espejo Welch, Cecile Hulog Cho, Marlene Soliven De Vera, Jocelyn Ayson Aquino, Virginia Barberan El-Sahn, Nora Cuison Salvatoriello, Dolores Asuncion, Evangeline Mangaliag Quero, Myrna Vitales Bautista, Rudy Calamiong

Back, l-r: Myrna Estrada Llorente, Connie Manalo Sural, Mary Ann Ocsan Lomibao, Teresita Lorezco Cuison, Gina Aquino Cadalin, Nicetas Castaneto, Josephine Pelias Villa, Jane Cambod Galo, Rosé Sahoy Sanchez, Carolyn Espino Espiritu, Susan Calica Hoffman, Rosalia Champay Salanga, Virginia Gumpeng

Georgina Aquino-Cadalin, '79

Roland Casem '79

Dolores Asuncion '79

Juliet Gaengan '79

Marlene Soliven De Vera '79

Nicetas Castaneto '79

Milagros Tiongson Mananquil, '79

Front, l-r: Thelma Limos, Reynaldo Reyes, Abraham Ragudos, Theresa Reyes Vidal, Avito Azarcon Jr, Roland Casem, Gloria Clifford

Back, l-r: Jane Torres, Blanca Dalaten, Helen Cabrito Camero, Vida Balbin, Marlyn Caloncagon, Shirley Pinera, Elena Daplian Canubas, Leonora Esperanza, Eva Aquino, Milagros Tiongson Mananquil

1979 - 2

1979 - 3

Front, l-r: Thelma Limos, Paula Socnayan Padcayan, Tina Siblagan Sadcopen, Blanca Dalaten, Leonora Esperanza
Back, l-r: Marlyn Caloncagon, Vida Balbin, Leonora Cerezo Mabutas. Theresa Reyes Vidal

Helen Camero
'79

Leonora Esperanza Beronia, 79

Marco La Madrid '79

Benjamin Quidangen '79

Reynaldo Reyes '79

Florence Trinidad '79

Rosemarie Sanchez '79

Abraham Ragudos '79

Avito Azarcon '79

Merlita N Manangan Class '79

Josephine Villa '79

Theresa Reyes Vidal, '79

Carolyn Espino Espiritu '79

Myrna Llorente '79

Mary Jane Torres '79

Teresita Lorezco Cuison, 79

Virginia Barberan El-Sahn '79

Jane Galo Class '79

Wilma Blount '79

1979 - 4

Front, l-r: , Benjamin Quidangen, Gloria Ditas Foronda Caballar, Candelaria Quisquisan Alera, Vivien Ballucanag Corpuz , Elena Daplian Canubas , Eva Aquino, Jane Torres , Lilia Dela Vega Angeles , Perseveranda Soriano Macaraeg, Nivas Lynn Bautista Nalundasan, Marco La Madrid, Romeo Tigno

Back, l-r: Helen Cabrito Camero, Gloria Clifford , Marlyn Abando Batan, Wilma Emily Bonsato Blount, Florencia Ganir Trinidad, Milagros Tiongson Mananquil, Juliet Gawe Gaengan, Merlita Manangan Zarate, Bernadette Manzano Saclolo, Lydia Pedro Abuan, Loida Ancheta

Bernardita Saclolo Class '79 | Rosalia Salanga '79 | Gloria Caballar '79 | Connie Manalo '79 | Shirley Pinera '79 | Jocelyn Ayson '79 | Myrna Bautista '79 | Vida Songcuan '79

Veronica Guillermo '79 | Candelaria Quisquisan '79 | Eva Santos '79 | Leonora Mabutas '79 | Cecilia Cho '79 | Marlyn Ubaldo '79 | Marlyn Batan '79

Blanquita Paras '79 | Rudy Calamiong '79 | Elena Canubas '79 | Evangeline Quero '79 | Marites Welch '79 | Virginia Tanacio '79 | Nora Salvatoriello '79 | Susan Hoffman '79

Vivian Corpuz '79 | Mary Ann Lomibao, '79 | Loida Macatol '79 | Lydia Abuan '79 | Lilia Angeles '79 | Nivas Lynn Nalundasan, '79 | Romeo Tigno '79 | Ricardo Rabot '79

1980s

Noemi Soberano
Busacay
Class '81

Marivic Guidangen
Falatico
Esther Jalandoni
Padernal
Marieta Corpus
Figueros
Class '82

Roland G.
Estigoy
Class '83

Quo Vadis BGHSNAAI?

The portals of the Baguio General Hospital School of Nursing (BGHSN) closed in 1984. There were only twenty-three graduates. Not one of them attended the recent international reunion of the BGHSN alumni association in Oct. 11-13, 2024, held at San Diego, California. There were also only five attendees from the early 1980s prior to BGHSN's closing – one from 1981, three from 1982, and one from 1983.

Question: Ten years from now, the 50th Golden Jubilarians will be the 1984 graduates. With their showing or none showing at the recent reunion, could we count on their sparse number to be a vanguard, celebrating their Golden Jubilee, in having an international reunion in 2034 – albeit to celebrate the life of the BGHSN?

Whatever might be true, Bienvenida Cristobal, with Class '69 and former instructor, points out, "However, the legacy of BGHSN continues to thrive through its Alumni. Unfortunately, as time passes, we cannot predict how long this legacy will endure, as our graduates are aging and, following the natural cycle of life, will inevitably pass away.

The recent international alumni reunion at the Marriott Marquis in Marina, San Diego highlighted, that despite the decreasing number of Alumni due to age and health issues, the camaraderie among BGHSN graduates remains strong."

With the rate of the BGHSN having reunions in a space of two or three years (discounting the COVID years), there could still be two to three reunions in the coming decade up to 1984. Continuing after the decade, there could still be reunions with no golden jubilarians at the helm. There could be diamond jubilarians starting in 1961 if the batches are able or are sponsored by the later years. More than likely, with the strong showing of the 1970s batches in the recent San Diego reunions, they will be the backbones of such diamond reunions with the earlier and later decade batches at the fringes.

And the reunions will go on until the attendance will dwindle and end sometime in the middle of the 21st Century.

However, memories will linger on in the annals of the Baguio General Hospital in general. Yes, we did have a BGHSN down there, at the west roadside of the Hospital. The memories of the alumni will be uttered by their relatives. Yes, my mom, grandma, or great grandma (and males, too) was a nurse graduate of the BGHSN. Memories could linger in reunion books, such as the ReminiscenceS, flipped by future generations and stories of reunion memoirs.

Albeit we thank the BGHSN that produced these nurses.

Top photo shows late President Elpidio Quirino, extreme left, visiting Baguio General Hospital led by then Hospital Director Dr. Justo Rosales. Looking on from behind of the cloaked nurse, was then Hospital Supervisor Eusebia Cariño-Luczon of BGHSN Class 1934. Above photo shows former staff of the BGH and BGHSN. In front, third from the right is former BGHSN Principal Clotilda Leung Tom. Behind her is Mrs. Eusebia Cariño-Luczon. Both photos were taken circa 1948.
-From the archives of Dr. Arturo Luczon -

For the record, the largest attended BGHSNAAI reunion was held at Baguio City, Philippines, in 2019, where, not including guests, 420 alumni attended. The largest, so far, reunion in the US was held at San Diego, California in Oct. 11-13, 2024. The last Golden Jubilarian reunion will be held in 2034.

The Last Golden Jubilarians

The Class '84 with Mrs. Liwayway Luczon, the class adviser.

The last Alumni Golden Jubilee Celebration with Class 1984 will be held in 2034. It will also be a celebration of the life of the Baguio General Hospital School of Nursing

Questions now:
When?
Where?
Who will Sponsor and Organize?

The First BGHSNAA International Reunion

Warnico Calica
Class '63

The first BGHSNAA International reunion was held in Chicago in July 17-19, 1992. Here is what Warnito Calica of Class '63 and one of the organizers said (encircled in the Officers page of the reunion's souvenir) about that reunion:

"I have attended so many reunions, but I vividly remember the first one in Chicago since we spent 2 years in planning with many arguments and laughter. We started with the intention of having a Christmas party for Chicago alumni only. In subsequent meetings, we expanded to Chicago and suburbs - State of Illinois, Tri state of Illinois, Indiana, and Michigan.

At further meetings we decided to go national and international. We mailed over 1000 invitations with self-address stamped envelopes. We pulled it off. There were tears of happiness, tears of sentiments, tears of satisfaction. We achieved a data base of BGHSN alumni that was eventually used by host associations.

It was hard work since we did not use email and cell phones then. Moreover, all of the planning committee members were working full time with different days off and shifts.

You have done well BGHSNAASC planning committee and its leaders for your diligence, commitment and determination to host the 12th BGHSNAA International Grand Reunion. Congratulations for a job well done and I am personally pleased with your efforts. I AM HAPPY TO SAY THAT YOU HAVE TRULY EXCEEDED MY EXPECTATIONS AND I AM GLAD THAT I ATTENDED THE REUNION. One of the best, second only to the First Grand reunion (of course I am prejudiced)."

Three Events of Fun in One Reunion

Roaring 20s Welcome Night

Marriott Marquis
San Diego, California

Gala Night

Marriott Marquis
San Diego, California

Picnic

Embarcadero Marina
Park North
San Diego, California

PROGRAM
Welcome Night
October 11, 2024, Friday
2:00 PM-5:00 PM – Registration, San Diego Ballroom
5:00 PM-11:00 PM – Program, San Diego Ballroom
Attire: Roaring 20s - Gatsby Era

Mistress and Master of Ceremonies
Connie Salaza Asiong, Cl '69 & Robert Villa, Cl '71

National Anthems **Joanne Baduria & Zeny de Guzman-Razalan Cl '69**
Star Spangled Banner & Pambansang Awit

Invocation **VEvilia Martin-Liganor, Cl '59**
Welcome Address **Thelma Mayo-Velbis, Cl '70**

BGHSN School Song

Florence Nightingale Walk **Arsenia Gonzales-Smith, Cl '77**
BGHSN Alumni **Merle Espiritu Arceo, Cl '77,**
Abraham Ragudos, Cl '79
Special Number **BGHSNAASC Officers & Planning Committee**

Buffet Dinner

Introduction of Celebrity Guest **Elizabeth Monroe Hamada-Platt, Cl '74**
Celebrity Performance **Rob Monroe Schneider**

Class Presentations & Talent Show

Dance **Cl '82 - led by Marietta Corpuz-Figueros**
Dance **"Flowers" by Cl '76 led by Aurora Boado-Manrique**
Ukelele Solo **Cl '76 - "Hukilao" by Susan Guzman-Castro**
Waltz Dance **Cl '79 East Coast & SoCal Group**
Led by Helen Cabrito-Camero
Gangnam Senior Citizens Line Dance **Cl '70 Led by Remedios Rivera-Go**
Dance – "Singing in the Rain" **Cl '74 Led by Cory Francisco-Edrozo**
Announcements **Connie Salaza Asiong Cl '69**
Opportunity Drawing **BGHSNAASC Logistics Team**

DANCE to the Music of DJNRY Productions

Snapping moments at the Roaring 20s

PROGRAM
Gala Night
October 12, 2024, Saturday
Theme: Living the BGHSN Legacy

1:00 PM - 4:00 PM - Photo Shoot – Torrey Pines Room
4:00 PM - 5:00 PM - Registration and Reception, Cocktails – San Diego Ballroom Foyer
5:00 PM - 12:00 AM - Program and Dinner - San Diego Ballroom

Mistress and Master of Ceremonies
Connie Salaza Asiong, Cl '69 & Robert Villa, Cl '71

Color Guard Parade	**Naval Medical Center San Diego**
National Anthems	**Joanne Baduria & Zeny de Guzman-Razalan Cl '69**

Star Spangled Banner & Pambansang Awit

Invocation	**Theresa Reyes-Vidal, Cl '79**
Welcome Address	**Crisabel Tabeta-Ramos, Class '74**
Inspirational Talk	**Carrie Buyao-Ramos Cl '61, Past President 2008-2022**
Introduction of Keynote Speaker	**Tess Gaetos, Cl '61**
Keynote Speaker	**Marietta Herrera-Gaddi, Cl '61**

Musical Entertainment/Montage

Presentation of Jubilarians

Ruby	**Class 1984 (40 years)**
Sapphire	**Class 1979 (45 years)**
Emerald	**Class 1969 (55 years)**
Diamond	**Class 1964 (60 years)**
Roll back Jubilarians	**Class 1971's 50th Anniversary (2021)**
Golden	**Class 1974 (50 years), Class Presentation**

Dinner/Music Entertainment by Joanne Baduria
Posthumous Recognition to Dr. Teodoro C. Arvisu-Founder BGHSN, 1922

Cultural Presentation	**Samahan Fil-Am Performing Arts & Edu Center**

Missions & Projects

Shunt for Life	**Melecia E. Madrid, Cl '67 & Zeny F. Bersamira, Cl '69**
Share-A-Grain	**Nora Cuison-Salvatoriello, Cl '79**
Adopt-A-Health Center	**Class '79**
Closing Remarks	**Nida Sotto Cristobal, Cl '69**

BGHSN Alma Mater Song

DANCE to the Music of DJNRY Productions

Welcome to the Gala

PROGRAM
Picnic Day
October 13, 2024, Sunday

10:00 AM - 5:00 PM - Embarcadero Marina Park North

Mistress and Master of Ceremonies
Connie Salaza Asiong, Cl '69 & Robert Villa, Cl '71

Picnic set-up
Food set- up; Arrival/Registration of alumni and guests
Band set-up
Park Rules – Connie S. Asiong
Grace before meals - Tess Gaetos, Cl '61
Lunch catered by Porky's Lechon & BBQ
Bidding for the next venue and host for the 13th Grand Reunion - 2026
Acknowledgements
First Alumna to Register – Merle Espiritu-Arceo, Cl '77
Class with the most attendees – Cl '79
Most Senior Attendee - Rosita Serdenia-Cabula, Cl '56
Alumni from other countries - Philippines, Guam, United Kingdom, Canada, Australia
Band Music & Surprise Number – Courtesy of Thelma Mayo-Velbis, Cl '70
After Care by all BGHSNAASC Officers & Committee Members
Closing
Games by Connie Salaza Asiong, Cl '69

Farewells and Well Wishes,
Till We meet again!

Welcome to the Picnic

The food was late, the line was long, it was hot but not even the diabetics complained. It was just a sumptuous meal with glorious fun with colleagues!

Happy to serve!

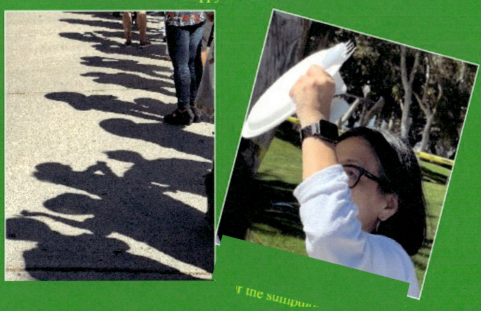

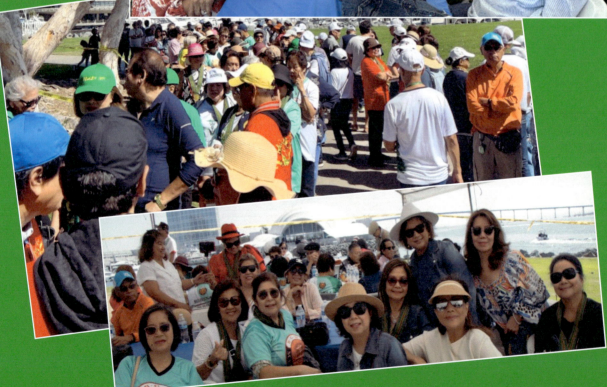

"And now, presenting to you.."

"Emcees are essential for keeping the audience engaged and making the event a success!
It's about more than just confidence or a strong stage presence; it's about captivating the audience.
Connie Asiong and **Robert Villa** embody these qualities perfectly!
Again, congratulations to both!" - *Nida Cristobal*

But ...Wait..

Where did he come from...?

Kudos Manuel R. Valerio Jr Cl 1963 for the wits and the fun.

...and the booties shook!

"The Last Waltz Dancers" L-R: Marites Espejo Welch, Benjie Quidangen, Milagros Tiongson Mananquil, Anthony Bautista, Myrna Vitales Bautista, Nora Cuison Salvatoriello, Armand Salvatoriello, Elena Daplian Canubas, Darwin Cannubas, Dolores Asuncion, Roland Casem

Getting a 'gold medal' for performing in a Talent Show during the Welcome Night of the BGHSNAAI Grand Reunion is like winning the lottery at that moment! Although this medal doesn't have the value of real gold—it was specially ordered from a Trophies/Medal Company—receiving it during such an important international reunion is truly special. Being recognized makes us feel appreciated and shows us that we matter. It boosts our spirits; we feel happy, supported, and inspired when recognized! Hence, keep it as a souvenir of the 12th BGHSNAAI Grand Reunion in San Diego!

The *'Payong'*

and *'Tungkod'* shows

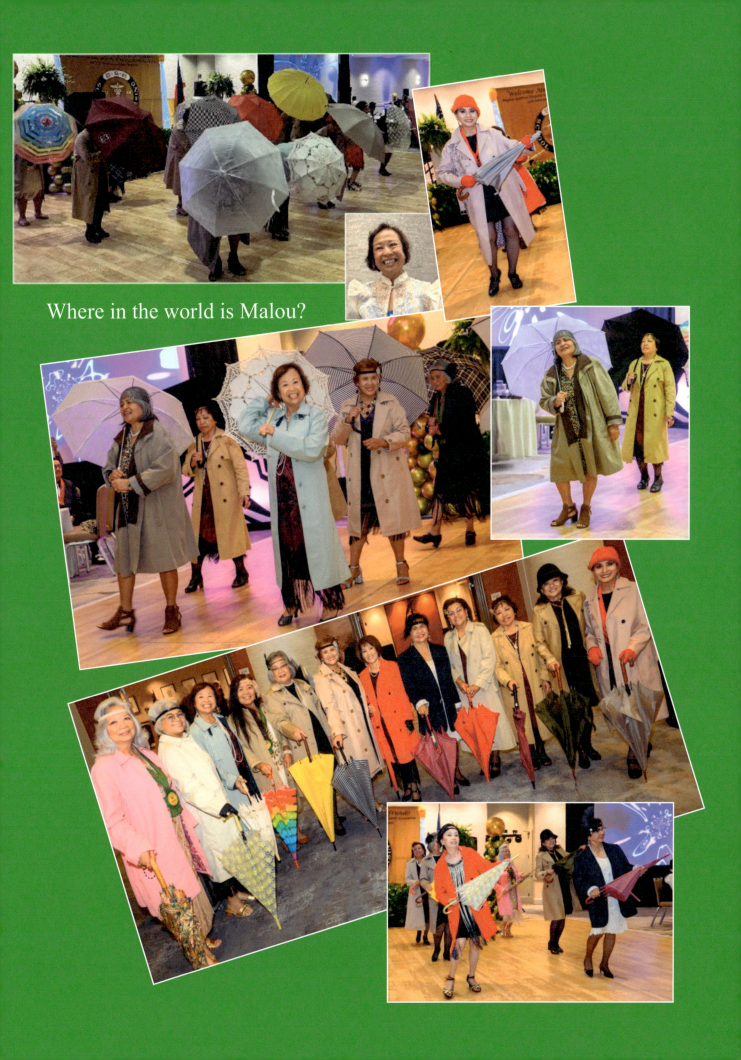

Where in the world is Malou?

A tinge of Cordillera Moves

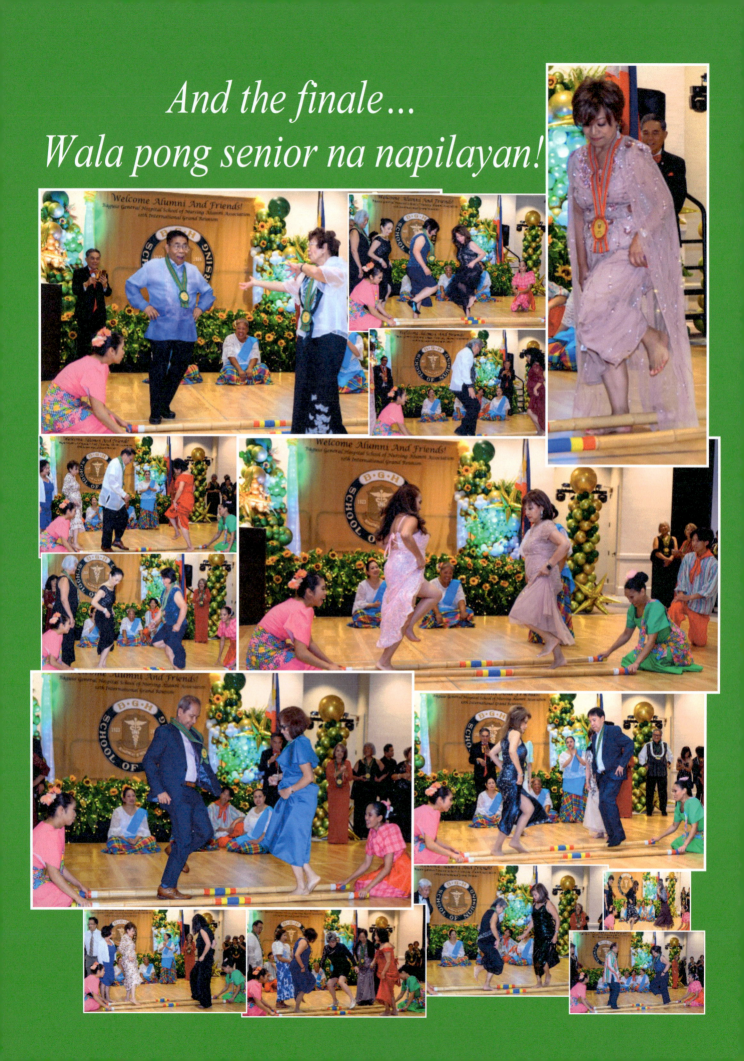

Can you still hear the music?

It lingers, doesn't it?

Worth Mentioning

Sising

A BGHSN Graduate Vignette Story

Getting the phone from her daughter who answered initially and gave her the phone, she said, "Hello."

It took me nanoseconds to respond as I was expecting a more elderly's voice. "Hello," I said. "I wanted to talk to Crescencia Vinluan, please."

"This is she," she said. "How may I help you/"

Again, I wondered to myself. Is this really she? The sound of her voice was not agreeing with the elderly woman's face and stature who was mingling with the younger nurse alumni at the picnic at the Embarcadero Park in San Diego, California. It was the last day of the Baguio General Hospital School of Nursing (BGHSN) alumni reunion last October, 2024.

I did not hear her talking at the park because she was at a distance amidst a sea of alumni and I was with my wife's circle of former students and co-instructors.

Now, talking over the phone, she did not sound raspy. There was no sense of trembling or hoarseness in her voice. Instead she sounded vibrant and brisk.

And she cracked jokes. "When my daughter said you wanted to talk to me, I thought you were with the FBI and I wondered what I must have done; or a scammer who would try to extort money from me."

Learning, that I was in the reunion and with The Aftermath to produce a 'book treasury chest of memories' about the three day event, she assumed I was also an alumnus. "So what class are you in?" she asked.

"I am not a BGHSN graduate, Manang Sising," I said. "My affinity with the school rests with my wife being a former clinical instructor there from 1975 to 1979."

She started asking me more questions which reflected her interest in people. I had to say, "Manang, this is not about me. This is about you."

I was barely two years old when Crescencia Manlongat Tamayo Vinluan graduated in 1953. She muses at the fact that she was not able to attend the first night events of the reunion but was so excited to have attended the picnic upon the prodding of Rosita (Sedenia-Cabula of Class '56). "I hoped that I would meet others that I know. Instead, more than half of those there were not even born yet when I graduated.

Only four,

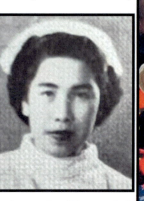 

excluding Vinluan, from the 1950s attended the first two previous nights' events.

"Nevertheless, I was so happy to mingle with so many nurses who are so enthused. I was so excited to be with those, who like me, were graduates of an institution we should all be thankful for and proud of. Did you know that during our time, the BGHSN was renowned to always have 100% passing in the Philippine Board Exams."

Known for her nickname "Sising,' she briefly worked in Dagupan City, her hometown, in the Philippines after her graduation.. In 1957, to upgrade her nursing skills, she acquired a student visa and had post graduate studies in New Jersey. Specializing in OB-Gyne - Labor and Delivery, she worked part time at the Margaret Hague Hospital, while pursuing her higher studies.

When already equipped with her chosen specialization, Sising moved to Toronto, Canada where her RN credentials from the Philippines were accepted by virtue of reciprocity.

Eventually, she would served in different hospitals in the mainland USA. She would end up being the supervisor of the Labor and Delivery unit at Coronado Community Hospital where she served from 1967 to 1995. Including her service in prior hospitals, Sising retired in 1995 after four decades of nursing service.

After her retirement, Sising continued visiting patients. She volunteered as a Eucharistic Minister with the St. Rose of Lima Church in Chula Vista in San Diego. This way she could visit patients in the wards of Scripps Hospital and join them in prayers. She even visited patients in their early days of being home with their babies.

She ministered patients along with her husband as her driver. She only stopped after five years when he got sick and succumb to the illness. "On Feb. 5, 2022, I felt the heaviness in my heart when I lost my sailor and my love," says Sising.

In an uncanny twist of circumstances, she had met her husband, Teofilo Vinluan, way back when she was still a nurse in the Philippines. She was then, on her own accord and without extra pay, visiting patients at their homes.

"His mother told me that he actually had a girlfriend already but every time I was there '*nagkakanakawan na kami ng tingin*' (we were already stealing glances at each other)," she said. "At that time, we considered each other just friends. Even our families became friends and my parents held him in high regards as he was a serious engineering student.

"That friendship was put on hold when I left for abroad. Every so often, we did write letters to each other. You could consider us being *penpals*.

"However, at the time that I was already in Canada, he joined the US Navy. The first time he docked here on furlough, already a sailor, he asked my parents where I was. Driving across the border, he tract me down. To make the story short, our friendship resumed and really blossomed into love."

Describing Teo, Sising says, "How can one not fall in love with this man. He was always determined and positive and loving with his thoughts.

"Nonetheless, I always kid, saying, 'the only reason you joined the US Navy is to be able to come to America and marry me.'" They had a hearty laughs with that line.

Teo and Sising married in 1963. The funny part was her parents, although they regarded Teo highly, they were adamant about him because of the saying that "navy guys had a woman in every port." His father went to every '*munisipyo*' in their province to check wedding registries. Finding that Teo was really single, they gave their blessings.

So, they got married and from then on, she followed Teo wherever he was deployed. She always found a nursing job wherever they were. These places would include, among others, New Jersey and Maryland.

Teo retired from service in 1996 after being with the Navy for 20 years. A year earlier, Sising had already retired as a nurse. They promoted themselves as grandparent baby sitters to their first grandchild.

They would eventually have five grandchildren - three from their son, Bernard; and two from their youngest daughter, Caroline. "Agnes stays with me now." Bernard manages apartments. "I consider Caroline as an extension of my being a nurse. Aside from being a special education teacher, she is a vet because she loves pets."

Not much of a social function goer now because of having to have a walker, Sising and Agnes had informally organized a mother-daughter meeting group. "We would just converse about anything, but mostly on how to maintain our health and exercise our minds and keep fit.

="I could have attended the three day BGHSN reunion but I was only told about the picnic," she said "Nonetheless, I was so happy. I was also very homesick, seeing all those younger former nurses, and nostalgic about the nursing school where I graduated from and provided the academic and practical skills that I needed in my professional journey."

Ending our conversation, her parting words were still about health. She said, "You take care of yourself, ha! And don't get old.."

She spells her nickname now as Sesing which is different from Sising from her yearbook '53. "That is okay," she says. "As long as they are below the same face in a picture."

What quips from a lady who was born in the early 1930s. *rdl11292024*

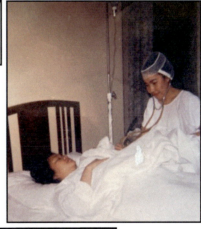

From top left, counterclockwise: Teofilo and Crescencia gets married in 1963; all at the Margaret Hague Hospital in New Jersey - at the nursery, facade of the hospital, and at the maternity ward, the Vinluans with their children from l-r: Caroline, Agnes, and Bernard.

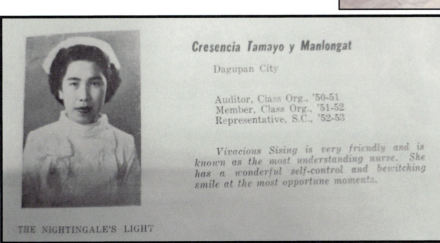

*It is worthwhile to note that how Crescencia (how her first name should have been spelled) was described in the yearbook of her Class 1953 embodies the 'Tender Loving Care" spirit instilled within the hearts of every alumni of the BGHSN. Every graduate of the School is imbued with the Nightingale's Light that glowed and glows in every corridor of medical facilities they have served and serve. **Source: BGH Archives***

"It was my mother's first social night out since my father died..."
—Rosalynn Valdez—

Rosita Serdenia-Cabula of Class 1956 with her late husband, Dr. Orlando Cabula.

We recently lost our dad, Dr. Orlando Cabula, in August 2024, barely two months before the reunion. Despite still grieving, our mom made the effort to attend the reunion. I, my husband, and eldest sister brought her to the function.

We are so glad we did. This was mom's first formal outing and seeing her happy, celebrating and mingling with all the nursing Alumni of BGHSN, was amazing. She was just too happy, seeing many nurses whom she remembered, and making new connections. We are beyond thankful and blessed that my mom attended this memorable event being the most senior graduate attendee. To all, continue to be amazing nurses and always remember your roots. As a nurse for 23 years myself, following mom's footsteps, I wish more power to the BGHSN Alumni and thankful to the Organizers for having a reunion that mom could attend.

— -Rosalynn Valdez-

A Reunion within a Reunion

1974

Nov. 15, 2016

Oct. 12, 2024

Crisabel Tabeta Ramos

Corazon Francisco Edrozo

Marissa Roaquin Javier

Eva Rodrigo Mamaril

Teresita Marrero Baterina

BFFs since their school days, from left to right, (and top to bottom graduates) Crisabel, Corazon, Marissa, Eva, and Teresita had been in contact with each other. Here is to Besties forever. See you together again in the next reunions

The Share a Grain and Adopt a Health Center Projects of the BGHSNAA - International

BGHSN Class '79 did not know that they would evolve into a humanitarian entity. They just started holding meetings in preparation for sponsoring the 11th BGHSNAA Grand Reunion held in Baguio City in Feb. 2019. The success of the reunion brought not only a congratulatory mold among them but a bond that would continue to foster unity and fellowship among them. Within those in the US mainland and those in the Philippines, they have formed an alliance of sort without really any particular goals except to keep in touch with each other made possible with the social media at hand.

Two years later, the deadly COVID-19 hit, sending the world into a standstill. This led to economic dislocations with the Philippines among the most stricken, sending more millions to poverty and want of basic necessities. Like a gust of wind, swirling within the heart of members of Class '79, there TLC tenets, morals and values came to fore.

With the beacon call to give back to the community where their alma mater, the Baguio General Hospital is, they asked themselves what they can do to help, in their little ways, those in distress, even just of a part of them.

Thus, evolved the group's 'Share a Grain' project upon the suggestion of Joseph Bondad. "*Nakakaawa nga yung mga nasa Pilipinas. Kung may bigas man sila, nilulugaw na lang nila,*" said Baguio General Hospital School of Nursing Alumni Association - International (BGHSNAAI) President Nora Salvatoriello. "We, here, in the mainland USA raised funds through service activities and by drawing from own bank accounts. The funds were channeled to our counterparts and allied groups in the Philippines" - specifically in Baguio City. "The counterparts also managed the purchasing and distribution of bags of rice to the identified indigents They did the leg work, even going to the barrios and coordinating with the barangay officers."

There would be four phases of raising funds, channeling, and distribution before the pandemic eased out. The project lasted for 22 months, serving 2,579 families coming from 53 barangays.

No less than Baguio City Mayor Benjamin Magalong commended the group's humanitarian reach to help alleviate the sufferings of indigents in the City during the crisis.

"We know that we could only do so much and would never be enough…but, at least, we are doing something and feel satisfaction for what we do," said Salvatoriello.

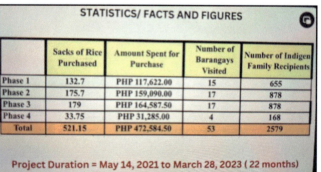

At left, BGHSNAA-International President Nora Salvatoriello updating the reunion attendees on their projects status and directions. Among other things, she made an impassioned call that projects have to be sustained and it will take funds to do so. They raised $2,392.00 that night.

STATISTICS/ FACTS AND FIGURES

	Sacks of Rice Purchased	Amount Spent for Purchase	Number of Barangays Visited	Number of Indigen Family Recipients
Phase 1	132.7	PHP 117,622.00	15	655
Phase 2	175.7	PHP 159,090.00	17	878
Phase 3	179	PHP 164,587.50	17	878
Phase 4	33.75	PHP 31,285.00	4	168
Total	521.15	PHP 472,584.50	53	2579

Project Duration = May 14, 2021 to March 28, 2023 (22 months)

The Evolution of the Adopt a Health Center Project

With the COVID-19 air clearing, but feeling great about their accomplishments with the Share a Grain project, the group groped for something else to do.

Referring to the members and allied groups, Salvatoriello said, "Ang dami-dami nila pinag-iisip hanggang, sa tulong ng mga taga-Baguio, nag-decide naming mag-adopt ng clinic or center."

"We were able to identify that the most needy center in Baguio was the Aurora Hill District Health Center," said Marco La Madrid, President of the allied groups based in Baguio City. "Although it is relatively a bigger clinic than most, it services 13 barangays with an aggregate population of 19,514 and the clinic is always short of supplies."

"To be able to buy these supplies, members pledged to contribute $10.00 a month which is only $120.00 a year," said Salvatoriello.

"Apart from what we purchased locally, those in the US also are able to gather needed medical paraphernalia to be sent to Baguio," La Madrid adds. "We have divided ourselves into who, per quarter, would be conducting surveys of what supplies are needed, purchase them, and deliver for the quarter they are needed.

"Starting next year, by the first quarter, specifically, March 2025, we would also be already donating supplies to a second health center. We are still identifying which one of two we have surveyed will be the recipient."

Top photo: The adopted center in Aurora Hill, Baguio City. Bottom photo: Plaque of Recognition presented to the BGHSNAA-International at the Reunion.

How the group evolved to be BGHSNAA - International

The BGHSNAA – International had its roots from being the BGHSNAA East Coast, organized mainly to prepare for the 11th reunion in 2019. The informal organization evolved into a nonprofit organization as a 501C3 registered entity. Benjamin Quidangen is the founding president and was succeeded by Nora Salvatoriello in the late 2022. The organization had to change the name, eliminating the 'East Coast' tag, because the other members - the backbone of which are from Class '79, are not from the region. Thus, they had to adopt 'International' so as not to restrict membership only from the East. They also have allies outside of the USA.

Civic Participations

Apart from their projects, the BGHSNAAI is also active in participating in activities of

BGHSNAA - International being recognized at the reunion - L-R: (BGHSNAAI Officers) Jane Cambod Galo, Helen Camero, Florence Trinidad, Marlyn Abando, Marlene Soliven De Vera, Gina Aquino-Cadalin, Vivien Ballucanag Corpuz, Marites Espejo Welch, Nora Cuison Salvatoriello, EmCee Connie Asiong, Ms. Marietta Gaddi, (from Phil.) Marco La Madrid, Wilma Bonsato Blount, Ditas Foronda Caballar, Paula Padcayan, Lydia Pedro, Loida Ancheta

the Filipino community in the East Coast. It is worthwhile to note that the husbands of Salvatoriello and member Marites E. Welch, Armand and Robert, respectively, are also very active in the organization, and along with the other spouses of the members, they also participate in shouting out for the BGHSNAAI.

Robert is also a nurse. A retired serviceman, he became a trauma nurse and transports critically ill patients in a helicopter. Armand is a retired engineer along the lines of titanium fabrication.

In such activities, emcees always announce the presence of the BGHSNAAI, saying in so many variant words, "Baguio City is the summer capital of the Philippines where the Baguio General Hospital School of Nursing Alumni Association originated and educated in Excellence in Nursing. The Baguio General Hospital School of Nursing Alumni Association International is a non-profit charitable organization that benefits the indigent and local communities in Baguio City and the surrounding communities of Benguet Province."

Continuing Commitment

"As long as we continue our commitment and have support from allied groups, we feel that we could make strides in sustaining our current project and expand towards other services," Salvatoriello said. "And we are expanding."

Although the backbone of the organization is Class '79, others, from different class batches, have also joined. "Many were especially inspired during the reunion," said Gina Aquino-Cadalin.

Cadalin, a member based in California, says, "As one of the Southern California officers, alongside with Marlene DeVera and Helen Camero, I feel a deep sense of pride being a representative of BGHSNAA-International. The vibrant spirit of an active member is not only limited to the officers but is shared among the entire batch of '79. It is inspiring

to see how the mentioned projects continue to flourish, highlighting the collective efforts of everyone involved, no matter how big or small their contribution. I am truly proud to be a part of this organization."

Salvatoriello also emphasizes, "Now that we have fixed ourselves, we feel that we should help fix others." *rdl12072024*

Photos - l-r to bottom:
Mr. And Mrs. Armand and Nora Salvatoriello; Mr. and Mrs. Robert and Marites Welch; Benjamin Quidangen being applauded for his leadership during the Share a Grain project; Armand and Robert always carry the banner of the BGHSNAAI banner whenever they have to join a community parade.

Shout out to the Baguio City based BGHSNAAI

Baguio allied members are the work force of the organization in realizing their humanitarian goal of giving back to the community. Baguio General Hospital School of Nursing, from where the members root their profession and success, was in the heart of the City. Nora Salvatoriello said, "Now that we have fixed ourselves, we feel that we should help fix others."

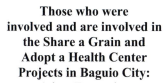

Those who were involved and are involved in the Share a Grain and Adopt a Health Center Projects in Baguio City:
Adora Fernandez
Annie Nicdao
Bernadette Angluben
Beverly Rose Tabra
Bonifacio Aquisan
Carlos dela Cruz
Deanna Mendoza
Delia Cabreros
Ditas Foronda
Elizabeth Huliganga
Elizabeth Serrano
Elizabeth Velasco
Fely Bugtong
Genoveva Corpuz
John Paul Lukas
Joji Calderon
Eusebio Palaganas
Lolita Torralba
Lydia Pedro
Ma. Loida Ancheta
Marco La Madrid
Mila Soria
Olivia Tiam
Ray Laroco
Sylvie Cominga
Teresa Moina
Wilma Bonsato
Leonila de Leon
Paula Padcayan
Leonila Cacho

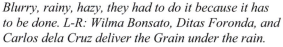

Blurry, rainy, hazy, they had to do it because it has to be done. L-R: Wilma Bonsato, Ditas Foronda, and Carlos dela Cruz deliver the Grain under the rain.

The Shunt for Life Project
-It used to be just a Dream-

It is mistakenly referred to as 'water in the brain' that makes the head, usually in younger children, grow into gigantic proportions. If left un-operated, it could be fatal for those afflicted.

Dr. Lauro San Jose, a neurologist surgeon, had a long-time dream of wanting to expel the 'water' from those affected for free. However, the operations would still entail costs in terms of surgical paraphernalia and post procedure-medicines to prevent infections.

For Dr. SJ, as affectionately addressed, the dream would have just remained as that – a dream. It broke his heart whenever he would meet parents who could not afford the surgery for their hydrocephalic children.

Hydrocephalus is a condition where excess cerebrospinal fluid (simply brain fluid and not 'water') is not excreted and trapped within the orbit of the brain, causing the head to expand.

Yes, it could have just been a dream unfulfilled.

In the most unlikely circumstance, however, he met Mel Madrid.

Madrid was on vacation with her family, including his dad, in the Philippines in 2000. In a freak accident, her dad, Julian Edra Sr., suffered a head injury that could have been fatal had he not been operated on by Dr. SJ, who was then on call. Although Edra would pass two years later due to another cause, the friendship between Dr. SJ and Madrid's family had become warm.

On a visit to the US, Dr. SJ, in a casual conversation, mentioned his dream of helping those hydrocephalic children, operating on them for free, but he needed help in terms of supplies and medicines.

In a flash, Madrid blurted, "Maybe we could help with that!"
After Dr. SJ had left, Madrid called her nurse '*amigas*,' and their friends. "*It was a mixed group*," Madrid said. She presented Dr. SJ's dream and "They were enthusiastic to help."

The Shunt for Life Project was born.

Zeny Bersamira was among those '*amigas*.' She said, "Yes from then on, we raised funds for what are needed for the surgeries. My husband, Tony, also got involved. We did it every year, going home to the Philippines, non-stop, even during the COVID years."

"Witnessing Dr. SJ operating on those children and seeing joyful hope in those parents' eyes are so self-actualizing," Madrid said. "The procedure involves putting a shunt tube at the base of the brain. The other end of the shunt is inserted into the stomach where the excess fluid is drained and excreted eventually."

Madrid adds, "Going home to do the missions is so addicting, and our member number is growing." We even have US doctors going home with us to assist local doctors in the Philippines aside from Dr. SJ.

Current BGHSNAA members of the project include: Tess Gaetos Class '61, Aurora Velasco '61, Mel Madrid '67, Jun Calima '68, Ping Calima '68, Josie Ruiz '68, Letty Carbonell-Ami '68, Lorna C. Baird '68, Ligaya Liwanag '68, Zeny Bersamira '69, Cora Gutierrez '71, Nida Quindara '70, and Remie Quiroz '70

The Shunt for Life celebrates its silver jubilee in February 2025 – a dream fulfilled and still going on with the help of BGHSNAA graduates and their friends. *rdl12102024*

For medical privacy reasons, we cannot name the patients. We also do not have before and after pictures because whenever the mission group goes back to the Philippines, it is hard to track down the former patients. It is suffice to say that over the 25 years that the Shunt for Life project has been going on, there are success stories that could be told about most of their former patients.

Top three photos: Dr. SJ operating on a patient, a severe case of a Hydrocephalus afflicted child; Left photo shows late BGHMC Chief Nurse Aurora P. Tenefrancia (second from right) visiting the mission participants; Top three pictures show - l-r: Tess Gaetos, Mel Madrid, and Lorna Casarino Baird cuddling post-op patients.

Shunt for life over the Years!

Ten-year-old former baby patient serenades the mission team.

Top and second rows show team members checking on post-op patients.

Bottom picture mission member receive Appreciation Commendations.

Shunt for Life Mission members pose during their trips over the years.

Mission members, patients with their parents and relatives in one of SFL mission trips.

A Voice from the Past

"As we shall go forth into the world, our lips will tell of the years as we shall look back to the precious moments with school friends the happy rapport with mentors who had altogether made us what we are."

Distinguished guests, members of the faculty, our beloved parents, members of the graduating class, ladies and gentlemen.

After three laborious years of study, hard work, patience and perseverance, it is presumed that we of the class 1963 are now ready to go out into the world scientifically informed, socially skilled, and technically competent to face a new challenge in our chosen profession.

Graduation, for all it means, should not be taken as a form of accomplishment for we are still far from being accomplished. Ours is only the beginning in this world of realities. Education has merely shed from our eyes the blinding influence of ignorance and has attuned us to the beautiful harmony in the universe of nature, man, and ideas. Titles and diplomas are merely objects or indications given for the purpose of providing us lasting reminders of our work. Verily, we, who are fortunate enough to have acquired education are presumed to be valuable assets in our country that evolves, accepts, and keeps faith with a system of improving herself.

The world ahead will be a bigger world and how we face our future will depend on how well prepared we are. It will be up to us to equip ourselves with the extra knowledge, added skills, attitudes and appreciations necessary to pursue our profession as nurses with responsibility, elegance, gentility, and respect. Nursing is peculiarly dependent on devotion for its quality - a devotion that is intense and selfless. It does not promise much for personal grandeur, social prestige or wealth in this seemingly materialistic world.

It is understandable that our sole objective is geared toward the concerted task of advancing the frontier of the religion of man: greatness, nobility and sanctity.

Our profession is a noble career - a humanitarian mission which requires the skill with gentle hands in ministering to the sick to ease their pains; the sense of duty and responsibility although it means the giving up of personal pleasures; the consecration to service by maintaining one's dignity and specially the love for fellowmen that can give only that inner peace and joy in return.

Eunice Bilagot Rios graduated valedictorian of Class 1963. This was her valedictory address. Her words then rings true to what BGHSN alumni went through in their professional life as nurses as nurtured with BGHSN.

As we leave behind our Alma Mater, we of the class '63 would like to express our sincerest appreciation and gratitude to the members of the faculty for having given our hand the needed skills…for having filled our hearts with confidence, understanding and determination: for the many pleasant years of association with our sisters of the lower classes. But most of all…to our beloved parents from whom we derive our inspirations. All these we shall not forget.

As we shall go forth into the world, our lips will tell of the years as we shall look back to the precious moments with school friends the happy rapport with mentors who had altogether made us what we are.

We shall strive to touch, to know the great common -human heart believing that here on earth, God's work must truly be our own.

Source: BGH Archives

10 Pairs of Sisters attended the Reunion

First Row, l-r

Marites E. Welch ('79)
Joy Espejo ('76)

Cecilia Herrera-Torres ('67)
Marietta Herrera-Gaddi ('61)

Mary A. Abiaro ('77)
Connie Asiong ('69)

Second Row, l-r

Alma D. Felmley ('70)
Cory Dizon ('72)

May Rose P. Quijano ('71)
May Alma P. Dy ('70)

Purificacion Sahoy ('76)
Rosemarie Sahoy ('79)

Third Row, l-r

Josephine M. Ruiz ('68)
Thelma M. Velbis ('70)

Rebecca R. Angeles ('69)
Virginia R. Bautista ('74)

Veronica Guillermo ('79)
Leony G. Gumabon ('76)

Bottom:
Cora Laranang Guevarra Class ('71)
Rose Laranang Belmonte Class ('74)

A Tribute to Clinical Instructors

Au Liporada, Liway Luczon, Nida Cristobal - Our dedicated teachers. -Blanca-

Forever young & beautiful. -Casa-

It sure was so nice to see you all. Thank you so much, Ma'ams. -Gina-

We're so happy to see all of you. You all look so great like when we were still students. -Nora-

It was nice seeing you, our instructors and mentors. Thank you for being a part of what I accomplished. I worked in a foreign land with no clinical experience in the Philippines. I just brought what I learned at BGH. I owe you and BGH for my professional success. Thank you. -Fona-

Ma'am Dada Cris, Au Liporada and Liway Luczon, you were all instrumental to what we turned out to be as professionals. Thank you and I hope we make you all proud. It was really inspiring to see you all. -Roland-

Love this. -Jean-

Seeing you all reminded me of my memorable days at our forever BGHSN. With grateful thanks to our instructors and mentors for those wonderful knowledge you imparted to us your nursing students of yesterday and now professional nurses. -

Yes…a lifetime to remember…i can't forget Ma'am Liporada at the dancing floor!!..full of energy!!thanks to our batchmate, Rey, for taking her out to show her moves…lol..love it! -Myrna-

Ageless beauties. -Bernadette-

Kagandahang walang kupas. -Ching-

The knowledge and skills I've learned from the three of you made me who I am today. Thank you so very much for the strong foundation you instilled in all of us that guided me until retirement day. I can say now that it is an honor to be a retired nurse. More power to the three of you. It was a pleasure seeing you again during our joyful 12th grand reunion. -Erlinda-

So nice and happy to see you all our dedicated teachers and mentors. Thank you for everything. Till we see you again. -Nicetas-

Clinical Instructors
Liway Luczon, Bienvenida Cristobal, Aurea Liporada

I would like to express my deepest gratitude to our BGHSN instructors - Ms. Bienvenida Cristobal, Mrs. Liway Lucson, and Mrs. Aurea Liporada. Your mentorship has been instrumental in shaping not only my career but also my growth as a professional. Through your guidance, you have shown us the true meaning of dedication, compassion, and leadership in the nursing field. Your support has paved the way for our success, and I am forever grateful for the opportunities we fearlessly faced. You have been a source of inspiration. We carried forward the values and lessons you've instilled in us. Thank you very much incredible teachers, mentors, and role models.
- Marites Espejo Welch-

Marites Espejo Welch
Class 1979

BGHSN has been my dream school as far as becoming a nurse. Since I was a 5-year old girl, the nursing uniform has enthralled me. The fulfillment of that dream came through the effective teachings of our mentors, instructors, and staff nurses. One such instructor is a smart, intelligent, efficient, and good nurse - Mrs. Aurea Liporada. She gave TLC its true meaning - not only in being a nurse, but, also in being a strong influencer on being kind, caring, and loving provider of excellent nursing care.
-Merle Arceo-

Irma Molina Ferrer, at left, thanks Mrs. Liway Luczon, her CI in Microbiology, when they were reunited after so many years.

Other former students also chimed in. **Janette N Ceferino Rivera** said, 'My best memory was when I challenged her in one of our exams that she labeled the parts wrong; and after I showed her the book, she conceded I was right; otherwise I would have probably flunked the test. **Marigold Guay** said, 'If not for you ma'am, I wouldn't be a nurse now.'

Dr. Teodoro C. Arvisu Awardees

In honor of Dr. Teodoro C. Arvisu, the founder of the BGHSN, the administration of the BGH School of Nursing established the Dr. Teodoro Arvisu Award in 1936. This prestigious award is presented to a graduating student who demonstrates exemplary performance in both academics and clinical practice during each Commencement Ceremony. At the 12th BGHSN Alumni Association International (BGHSNAAI) Grand Reunion, five distinguished Dr. Teodoro C. Arvisu Award recipients were in attendance, highlighting the honor's prestigious nature. This award is exclusively granted to class valedictorians. Among the notable attendees were guest speaker Marietta Herrera-Gaddi (Class of '61), Eunice Bilagot-Rios (Class of '63), Tomas Madayag (Class of '70), Vicky Ventura-Gumayagay (Class of '75), and Marivic Guidangen-Falatico (Class of '82). Their presence exemplifies the excellence and achievements recognized by this esteemed award. Congratulations to all recipients, and may you continue to excel! **-DadaCris-**

Veteran Instructors

Fifty-two years later, two nursing instructors from the Baguio General Hospital School of Nursing reunited at the reunion. Marietta Herrera-Gaddi, at left, taught Massage and Bandaging, while Deborah R. Bajada taught Surgical Nursing. Both were recognized as exceptional mentors during their time and continue to be admired today. Marietta is a BGHSN graduate in 1961. Deborah is an alumna of the UP College of Nursing. Mrs. Gaddi was the guest speaker, while Mrs. Bajada was a special guest. Meeting them at the reunion was a joyful and inspiring experience. -DadaCris-

Nothing Stopped them from coming

Inspite of their physical limitations, (l-r): Estrellita Padilla-Nerona; Arsenia Duldulao-Bulacan; Severina Alvendia-Salcedo, all of Class '62 attended the reunion.

Ading and Manang

Throughout my nursing education, having an Ate and an Ading was incredibly rewarding. I'm honored to have been among them. I have not seen my Ading since our graduation in 1979. Our reunion after 45+ years was a truly joyful moment.
This is just the beginning of more reunions. See you again sometime Ading Roland
-Gina Cadalin-

CIs Party, Too

The crowded dance floor did not deter former Instructors (l-r) Liway Luczon, Aurea Liporada, and Nida Cristobal from showing their moves. Per Nida, "We, three mentors, found the foyer a perfect place to showcase our dance moves- bending, rising, shaking, stretching, twisting, turning, and swaying. Despite the aches and pains that come with age, the enjoyment of the event was palpable. I'm so glad I survived that night!"

Wow!
"I became a PopCom Regional Officer," Vivien Corpuz Bacullanag, of Class '79, shares the early days of her professional journey with former BGH OB-GYN Dr. Arthur Luczon.

Really?!?
What was so hilarious during their past that former Instructors Aurea Liporada and Bienvenida Cristobal had to Burst into a guffaw with their former students?

She was *Voluntold*
Wala lang po. Nautusan lang pong maging Orchid Salesgirl si Mila Seguban of Class '62.

Cousins Reunited
ReminiscenceS Staff, Roy 'Saleng Ken Marapait' Reclosado, reunites with her cousin, Edna Rivera Gutierrez of Class '66.

ASIONG SIBLINGS- All RNs!
They all attended the 12th BGHSNAAI Grand Reunion @ Marriott Marquis Marina, San Diego, CA

Asiong Sisters - RNs ALL

Connie says, "Our dad, Jacinto Asiong, wanted his girls to follow in the footsteps of his cousin, the late BGHSN Principal Clotilda Tom. So, he strongly encouraged us to take up nursing. Mary and I (leftmost and rightmost at the left picture respectively), graduated from the BGHSN. Susan (left at right picture) finished from Virgin Milagrosa Nursing School and Junette (center at left photo), from SLU Nursing School.

Prettiest Faces

"They were considered two who had the prettiest faces of Class 1968 during their student days at BGHSN. And they have lived to that expectation to the present- Jane Tano-Sali and Marylyn Asprer-Lopez.
-Dada Cris-

Zendy Razalan

Zendy Razalan, daughter of Dr. Lee and Zenaida de-Guzman Razalan from the Class of 1969, is a vibrant presence at our class gatherings and BGHSNAA-SC meetings. With her warm and affectionate spirit, she delights everyone by calling them "Aunties" or "Uncles," while I am honored to be called "Mama," and Rebecca Ramos-Angeles is lovingly referred to as "Nanay."

Zendy is not just an attentive listener; she is a true volunteer at heart, consistently stepping up for tasks and excelling at them. Many of the individual photos of the BGHSNAA-SC officers showcased in the Reunion Book 2024 were brilliantly captured by her using her iPhone. Her tech skills surpass those of her mother, Zeny, making her an invaluable asset to our group. Whenever we have collaborative tasks, Zendy eagerly offers her assistance and quickly masters new skills to ensure everything runs smoothly.

We truly appreciate you, Zendy! Your contributions make our gatherings special!
-Dada Cris-

IDOL
We all enjoyed such an iconic reunion event through the leadership of this lady Connie Salazar Asiong. She was the first one we met when we entered the hall the first day and the last one we saw making sure everything was fine during the last day. I haven't seen anyone else who worked harder that she did. She was an Emcee, peace keeper, cheerer, and performer - all rolled into one - and did each one perfectly. And at the picnic, she was one of those who were left behind to make. After all that, she hurried to her car and, with a smile, said hello again. She is great! And she deserves a loud clap! -Joy Noe '74-

The Godmother - The last time I saw her was in my wedding 36 years ago. She is my primary sponsor and she is still the same, lovely; didn't aged at all. So happy to reconnect with you, Ninang!

Love at First Site

Life is undoubtedly beautiful. It's about giving and family. BGHSNAA is family to us. We were nursing students in the late 70s at the BGHSN, and that's where our love story and family began.

It's like, at that moment, the whole universe existed just to bring us together.

That universe included the enduring presence of our former classmates who became friends. Sustaining the connections through like attending reunions have always been a truly wonderful experience. They allow us to reunite and construct cherished memories together.

We eagerly anticipate the next reunions

Romeo Tigno, Cl'79
Florence Bigornia-Tigno, Cl'78

A Marites Session with Georgina Aquino-Cadalin, Class '79, at center

Oh! No. We are not talking about you.

We thank the Organizers for giving us the chance to bond, reminisce and have fun!

A murmur of sophisticated conversation flowed through the room, punctuated by lots of chatter, amusement talks and laughter. It was, in short, a truly memorable evening, a celebration of elegance and the joy of reconnecting and reminiscing.

Perla Bambico, Malou Sison, and Beth Platt of Class '74 in 1974 and 50 years later at the reunion.

Nightingale's light and BGHSN's TLC are alive with Arsenia and Merle.

Twins?

Normally, a woman hates it when someone else in a party is attired with the same dress as hers. Not during the reunion where Nora Salvatoriello, of Class '79, was as happy as Dinah Cilewicz, of Class '76, when they had the same Roaring 20s outfits. It was more the reuniting with co-BGHSN alumni that took precedent over vanity.

Nonetheless, online retailers must be thrilled to witness our alumni making such a positive impact on their brands! It's fantastic that many of our nurses chose their stunning Roaring 20s outfits for the Welcome Night.

Our alumni's beautiful styles created a sense of unity, with many looking like twins, triplets, or even quintuplets! This vibrant display highlights how our community cherishes nostalgia and proudly supports local businesses. It was a night to remember, celebrating great fashion and strong connections!

-Dada Cris-

Looking Back

Written in August 19, 2018 before the 11th International BGHSNAA Reunion for the Northern Dispatch by Aurea Liporada

I love reunions. They are hubs that remind me of who I was. Yes, they are reminders of my glorious past that could explain where I am now and where I could further be heading. Whether they are a gathering of family, classmates, town-mates, clubs, or simply friends, reunions provide a perspective of how one's present was shaped from the past and how one could redefine further one's future. This goes without saying that everyone in your past that you have interacted with and are part of whatever reunion you are in or will be has somehow contributed at least a pebble that has helped cement the pillar that you have become.

This coming January and February 2019, I will be attending four such reunions. Three with my husband's: with his Saint Louis Boys' High School Alumni, the Ex-Seminarians of the CICM, and the Beta Gamma Phi Fraternity and Sorority of the University of the Philippines – Baguio. No offense to my husband's reunion mates but what I am most excited about is the 11th International Grand Reunion of the Baguio General Hospital School of Nursing Alumni Association (BGHSNAA) on Feb. 15-17, 2019 in Baguio City.

Although I am not an alumna of the Baguio General Hospital School of Nursing (BGHSN), I was a clinical instructor there from 1975 to 1979. Having attended most of the school's past reunions, I always had the exhilarating feelings at re-bonding with my former students, former co-instructors; and forging bonds with their current families. Learning how my former students are living out in their fields, embued with the Tender Loving Care (TLC) as ingrained in them,

The hospital started as Baguio Sanatorium in February 3, 1902 pioneered by Dr. Eugene Stafford, captain of the staff of General Arthur MacArthur in the 1900's.

also sent gratifying feelings of pride in my heart at how I may have played a part, no matter how minute, in their journey in life. This goes without saying that I am also thankful to them for they have provided me with the necessary experience that helped me with my career advancements beyond BGHSN.

For that matter, I believe, we should be thankful to the Baguio General Hospital (BGH) as an institution in itself and not only for its school of nursing. The BGHSNAA is but an offshoot of BGH's humble beginnings with the humble beginnings of the City of Baguio itself. From an appropriation of mere Ten Thousand Pesos then, a sanitarium was constructed in March 27, 1902 where Pines Hotel used to be or where the present SM-Baguio now stands. The then 15 bed capacity evolved to become the Baguio General Hospital in 1937.

Recognizing the need for more nurses, the Philippine Congress passed a resolution in 1922 creating BGH's school of nursing. It opened the following year, 1923, with nine students. From then on, throughout the peaceful times and through the Japanese war, graduates fanned out from the portals of the school to render their Tender Loving Care virtue, not only for the patients in Baguio City, but throughout the farthest corners of the world.

It is worthwhile to note that the Class of 1945 had the most unique graduation exercise. Nine seniors graduated amidst interruption by American planes carpet-bombing the City. They also stayed to serve patients even if their lives were in danger.

And the Nightingale's light continued to shine on from the School of Nursing even in foreign lands.

I consider myself fortunate to be part of the School's latter history. More so because it closed its portals in 1984. After 61 years, it had produced 3,885 graduates. I am so proud to be privileged to have been part of four batches. I am so proud to have been part of an institution that had been true and continue to be true, through its graduates, to its mission of tendering the highest service with loving care to patients even at the most far-flung corners of the world.

Thus, I will make it a point, whenever I can, to attend all reunions of the BGHSNAA. I will do this knowing that if the school closed in 1984, the last dwindling reunions should be sometime between 2060's to the 2070's. I will do so…enjoying the camaraderie of my former students, alumna and alumni, co-instructors, their families, and other colleagues…with the thought that the Baguio General Hospital School of Nursing and how it prepared us to serve society will forever live in our hearts.

Aurea Liporada - RN-BSN, MM-Ed Adm - *is a graduate of St. Paul's University - Manila; with a Master's Degree from the University of the Philippines. Before becoming a BGHSN clinical instructor, she was a public health nurse with the Baguio Health Department. She was also an instructor at the Manila Central University, Arellano School of Nursing, St. Louis University School of Nursing, and Pines City Doctors' Hospital. Before immigrating to the US, she served as an instructor at the University Teaching Hospital School of Nursing in Lusaka, Zambia, Africa. She retired as an RN operating room nurse after serving 28 years at St. John's Hospital in Oxnard, California.*

Favorite Reunion Photos

Class '77   Class '78

Henry and Nancy 'Nan' Manuel Villa

Rollie and Nelly Dawana Reyes
Class '73

With Class '73 Batchmates

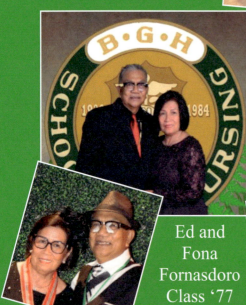
Ed and Fona Fornasdoro
Class '77

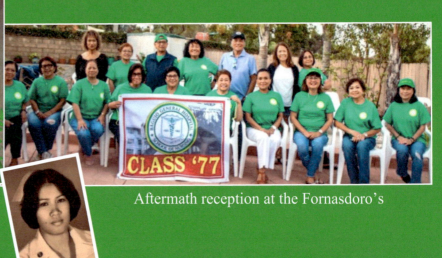
Aftermath reception at the Fornasdoro's

With Perla Bambico and Malou Sison in 1974 and 50 years later. - Beth Platt, Class '74

Georgina Aquino-Cadalin, Class '79

Paul and Elena O'Mary with Class '74 and with Cresentia Tamayo Vinluan of Class '53 and Rosita Cabula-Serdenia of Class '56

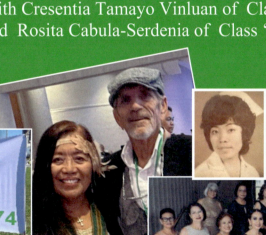

Doug and Jocelyn Noe Class '74

Malou Sison
Class '74

Cecilia Cho
Class '79

Caroline Calpito
Class '76

Rey and Carol Calpito

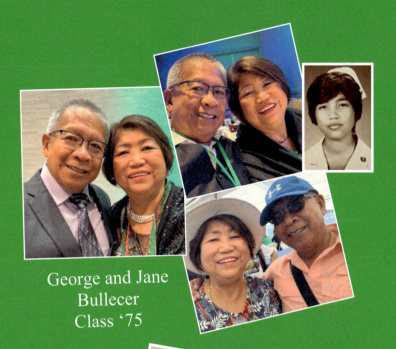

George and Jane Bullecer
Class '75

Art & Esther Bulayo
Class '74

With Rose Belmonte

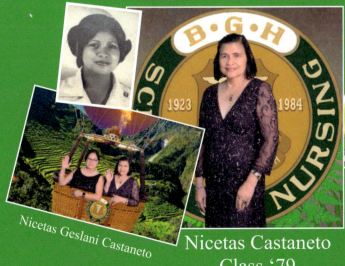

Nicetas Geslani Castaneto

Nicetas Castaneto
Class '79

With Nida Cristobal &
Mr. Eusebio Castaneto, Jr.

Roland Casem, Class '79
At far left is Maria Loida Ancheta

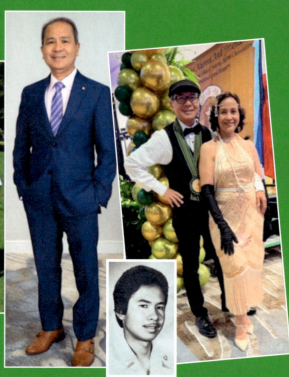

Noemi Soberano Busacay
Class '81

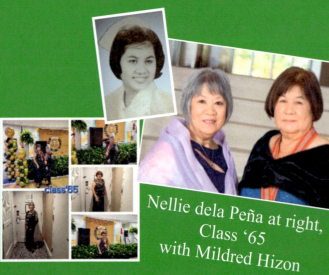
Nellie dela Peña at right,
Class '65
with Mildred Hizon

With Susie Macayan

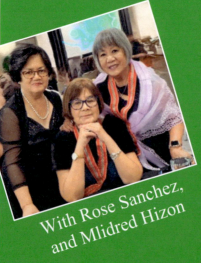
With Rose Sanchez,
and Mildred Hizon

Whelma Sales Nilo
Class '74

Dolores Asuncion
Class '79

Naty, Class '76,
with Husband,
Alex Savellano

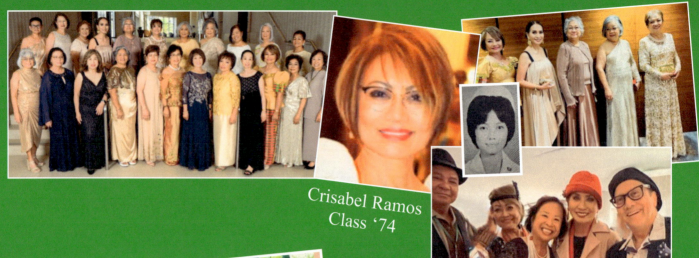

Crisabel Ramos
Class '74

Marlene Soliven De Vera
Cl' 79

CAROLYN ESPINO ESPIRITU

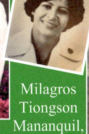

Milagros Tiongson Mananquil, Class '79

Cora Laranang Guevarra Cl'71 and Rose Laranang Belmonte Cl'74

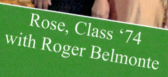

Rose, Class '74 with Roger Belmonte

Rose's sisters: Sr. Pacita Laranang, ICM Cl'63 and Corazon Laranang Guevarra Cl'71 respectively

At right, rightmost, Merle Arceo, Class '78 with Aurora Manrique, Class '76

Carmelita Ramos Domingo
Class '74

At right, Nora Cuison-Salvatoriello, Class '79
RN, MSN, CCRN, RN-C, NP-BC, ANP-C
President - BGHSNAA, International Inc.

Jovet Buenaventura Flores, Class '76

Virginia Barberan El-Sahn Class 1979

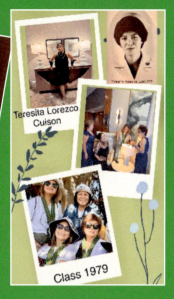

Teresita Lorezco Cuison Class 1979

Loreta, Class '78 with husband, Eduardo Bassig

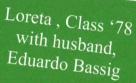

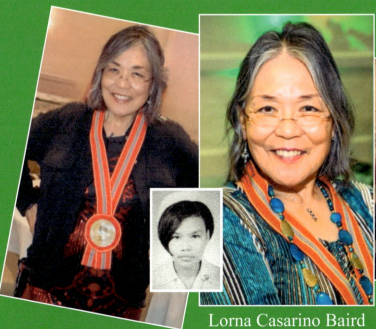

Lorna Casarino Baird Class '68

Aurora Manrique
Class '76

Alma Dizon Felmley of Class '70, second from right, with (l-r) Cecilia Herrera Torres of '67, Cory C. Dizon of '72, and Dr. Marietta Herrera Gaddi of '61 and guest speaker at the reunion.

Alma Dizon Felmley
Class '70

Teresita Gaetos
Class '61
with her batchmates

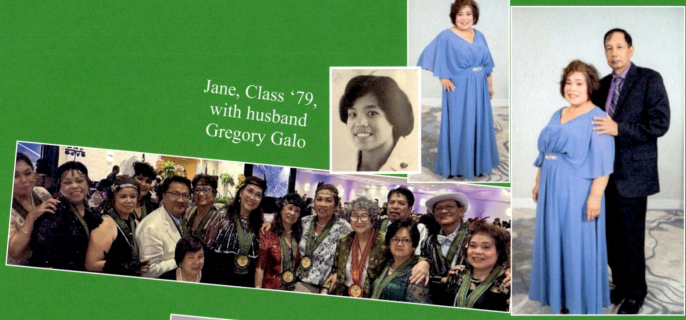

Jane, Class '79, with husband Gregory Galo

Marivic Guidangen
Class '82

Merlita N Manangan
Class '79

Marylyn Asprer-Lopez, Class '68

Percy Soriano Macaraeg
Class '79

With Nora, at left, and Candy, at right, also of Class '79

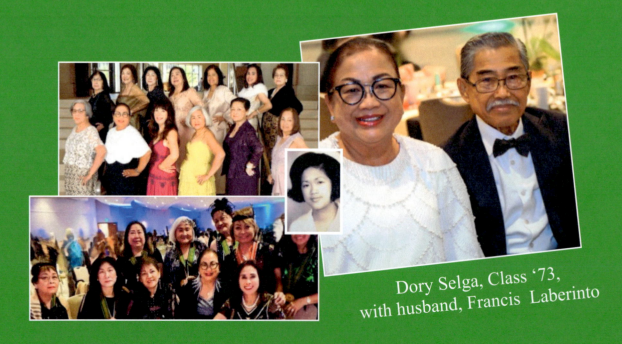

Dory Selga, Class '73,
with husband, Francis Laberinto

Teresita Marrero, Class '74, with Dodo Baterina

Eva Manlongat-Arnoldi, Class '69 with her batchmates

With Alma D. Felmley '70

Cory C. Dizon, Class '72

With Alma D. Felmley '70

Virgie R. Bautista
Class '74

With batchmate Josie Mejia

Eva Rodrigo Mamaril
Class '74

Emy, Class '74
with Ador Pinera

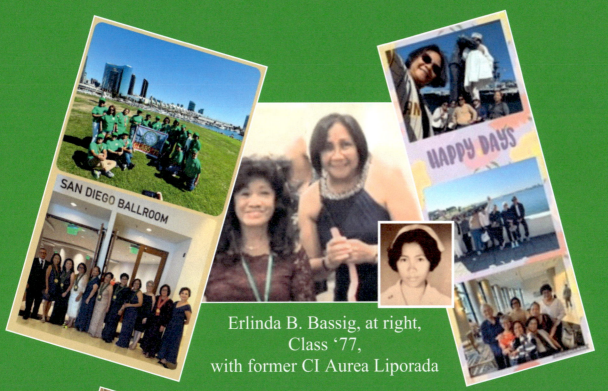

Erlinda B. Bassig, at right,
Class '77,
with former CI Aurea Liporada

Nellie Bumanglag Alcon
Class '74

Josephine Villa, Class '79

Josie Ruiz, Class '68

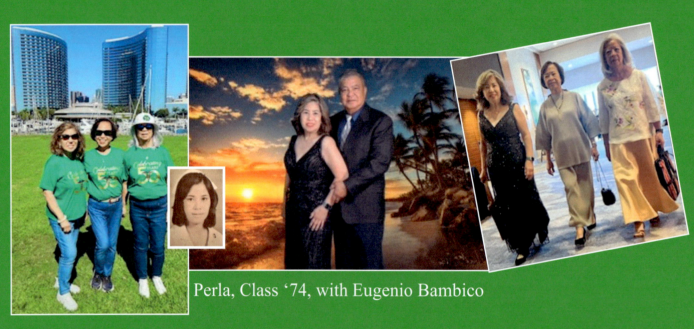

Perla, Class '74, with Eugenio Bambico

Jane Tano Sali, Class '68

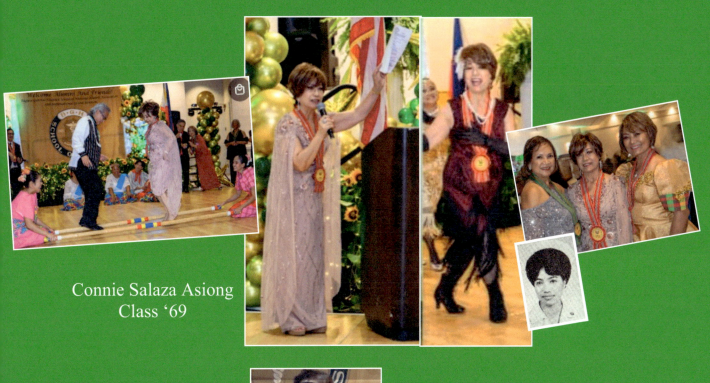

Connie Salaza Asiong
Class '69

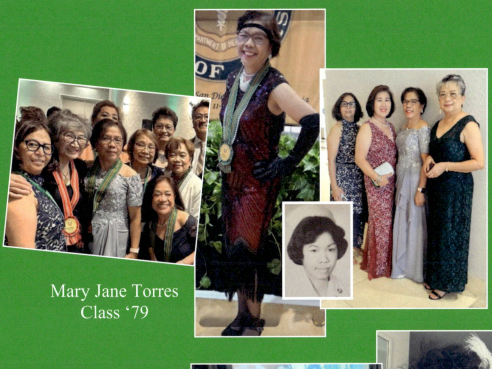

Mary Jane Torres
Class '79

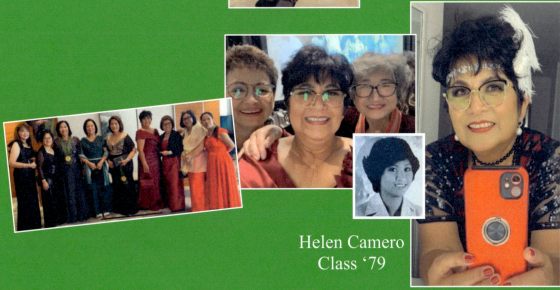

Helen Camero
Class '79

Josie Mejia
Class '74

Wilma Emily Bonsato-Blount
Class '79

Myrna Llorente
'79

Myrna Labonete Boontiang,
Class '79

With Carol David Macaraeg

Elsa, Class '74
with husband,
Ruben Salazar

With Tish Marrero Baterina
and Esther Copero Bulayo

Rebecca Angeles, Class '69
with Enrique Juson

Back Row: Dr. Ramon Lopez, Marylyn Asprer Lopez, Nerisa Lagatao Tabora, Dr. Mark Spiro
Front Row: Lorna Casarino Baird, Josie Mayo Ruiz, Jane Tano Sali, , Lolita Flores Spiro

With Menzie Clarke

With Jane Sali, Marylyn Lopez, Josie Ruiz, ,Lolita Spiro

Nerisa Lagatao Tabora, '68

Corazon, Class '74, with husband, Johnny Edrozo

Vivien Ballucanag-Corpuz Class '79

Gloria Ditas
Foronda-Caballar
Class '79

Ma. Loida Ancheta
Macatol Class '79

Bernardita Saclolo
Class '79

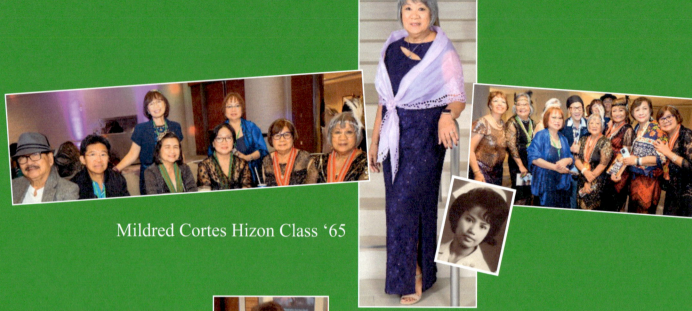

Mildred Cortes Hizon Class '65

Concepcion 'Ching' Egmin Magalued, Class '77 with husband, Alexander G. Magalued

Myrna Bautista, Class '79

Alicia Delacruz Doria
Class '71

Evangeline Mangaliag
Quero, Class 79

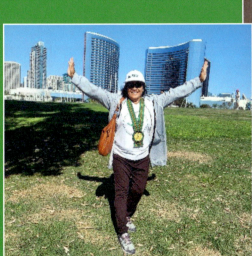

Florence Ganir Trinidad
Class '79

Arsenia Gonzales Smith, Class '77, with husband, Frank Smith

Marco La Madrid, Class '79 with Dory La Madrid

Mary Ann Ocsan Lomibao
Class '79

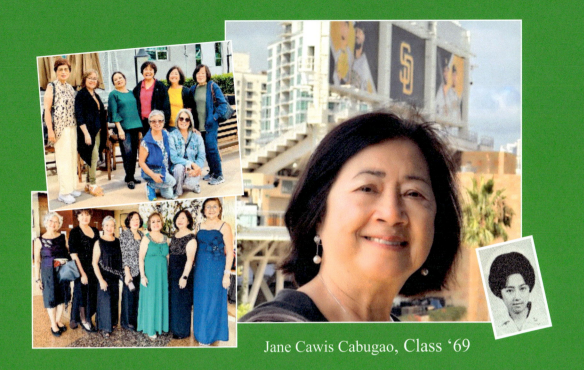
Jane Cawis Cabugao, Class '69

Rosita Serdenia Cabula, Class '56

Norma Tadina, Class '77 with husband, Amado Guanzon

Susan Castro, Class '76

Milagros Rimando Largo, '69

Avelina Dulay Estepa, Class '73

Irma
Molina
Ferrer
Class '76

Josephine
Espino
Abalos
Class '76

Zeny
Bersamira
Class '69

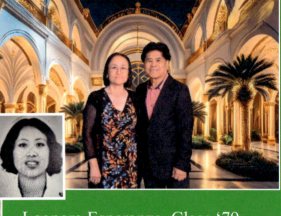

Leonora Esperanza, Class '79, with husband, Pepe Beronia

Ricardo Rabot, Class '79

The ReminiscenceS Favorite Photo and Statement

"I'm thrilled that I brought Yolly, my wonderful wife, to my alumni reunion. It's a perfect opportunity for her to see how lucky she is to have chosen me as her lifelong partner." - **Rolly Estigoy Class '83**.

Thank you for a memorable reunion from all us!

Dolores Asuncion

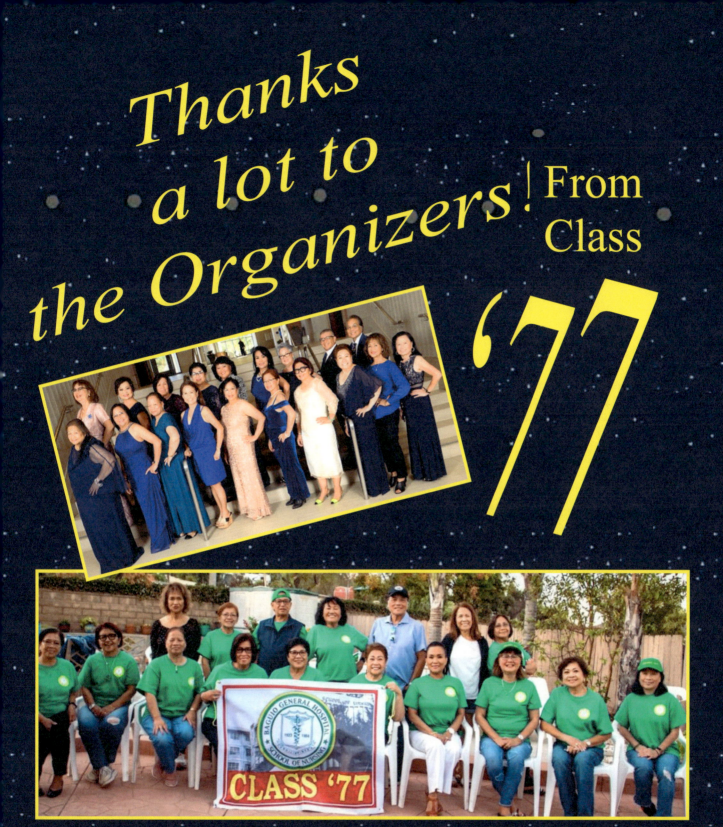

Thanks a lot to the Organizers! From Class '77

Seated, l-r: Elenita Timbuloy-Carlos, Juliet Abalos-Pulicay, Arsenia Ramos-Gayomba, Fona Raguro-Fornasdoro, Helen Aoay-Ayeo, Ching Egmin-Magalued, Celia Cabigas-Darrow, Norma Tadina-Guanzon, Arsenia Gonzales-Smith, Julita Untalan-Imus
Standing, l-r: Virginia Esperon, Mary Asiong Abiaro, Henry Fine, Eden Jaravata-Strutner, Henry Villa, Elvira Gonatice-Bautista, Erlinda Bassig

It was an unforgettable Reunion!

Arlene Lumanlan
Aurora Boado Manrique
Divine Guerrero

Purification Sahoy Serna
Myrna Talento Garcia
Erminda Torralba Alonso

Naty Rimorin Savellano
Leonarda Gumabon
Edna Belen Rodriguez Adviento
Susan Guzman

Lillian Calamiong Corpuz
Caroline Gomez Callisto

Class 1976

Dinah Imbat Cilewicz
Jocelyn Espejo
Brenda Tamayo

Jane Galpo Pacalso
Jovet Buenaventura Flores
Flordeliza Cabatic Radam

Josephine Espino Abalos
Cristina Yapyap Lao
Carmela Postadan
Judith Ponsones-congjuico

Teresita Peralta Saludares
Irma Molina-Ferrer

Our Heartful Thanks to you.
We reminisced, we mingled. we danced, we sang, we broke into laughter. We had fun, we will have memories of this Joyous Reunion to treasure. All because of your great efforts. We are forever grateful to the Planners and Organizers. From:
Class '76 Attendees

Thank you for the Reunion & the Reminiscing Exuberance

From
Aurelia Medrano
Manganilo
Class 1973

More Power
To the
BGHSNAA!

Thank you for a memorable Reunion.

Dory Selga Laberinto
Class 1973

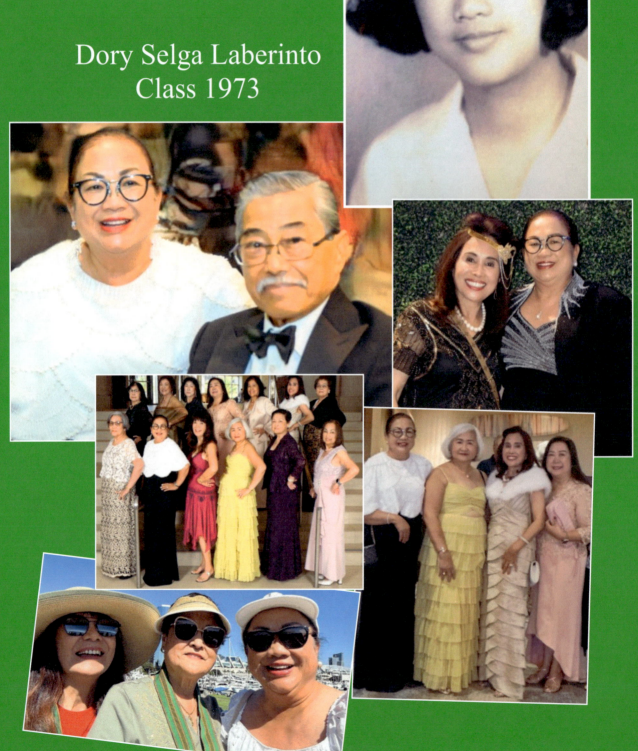

Mabuhay and Thanks to the Organizers of the Wonderful Reunion!

Fe Antonio
Class '73

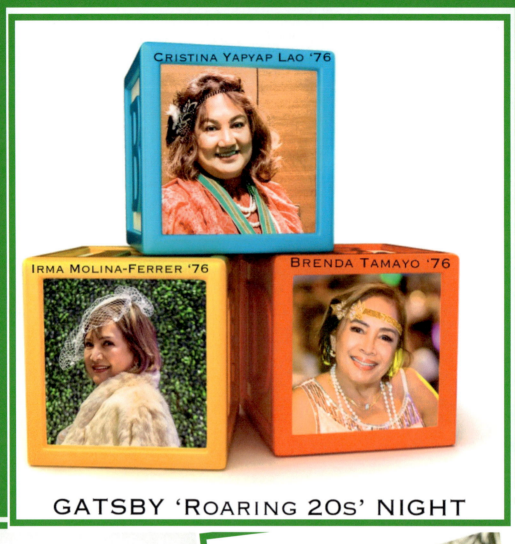

GATSBY 'ROARING 20s' NIGHT

GALA NIGHT
OCTOBER 12, 2024

(L-R) Brenda Tamayo, Irma Molina-Ferrer, Cristina Yapyap Lao

SAN DIEGO EMBARCADERO NORTH 'PICNIC'

Thank You for the Jubilation!

*Thank You
for a wonderful reunion
which gave us a chance to
bond with our former classmates
and other BGHSN Alumni!
Kudos to the Organizers!*

Lillian Lachica
Ancheta
Class '73

BGHSN Class 1973

Nelly Dawana Reyes
Class 1973

Thank you
BGHSNAA
Southern
California
for a
well orgnized
Reunion!

We had a wonderful time in frolic while bonding with former classmates and colleagues. Thank for all Your efforts, BGHSNAA Southern California!

Primrose de Leon Joaquin
Class 73

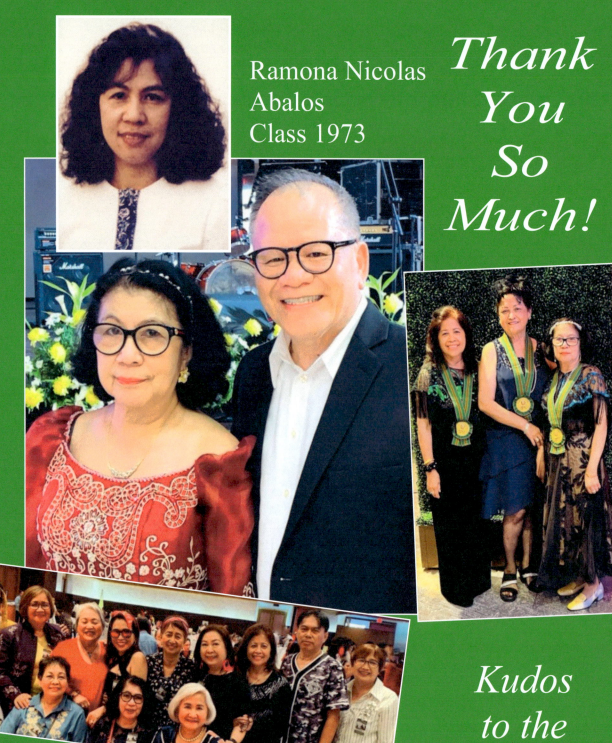

Ramona Nicolas Abalos
Class 1973

Thank You So Much!

Kudos to the Organizers for a job well done!
-Class '73-

Thank You for the Reunion!

Susan Guzman Castro
Class 1976

*Our Family
thanks the Organizers
for our bonding
with former classmates
who are now our colleagues!*

Trifona Raguro Fornasdoro
Class '77

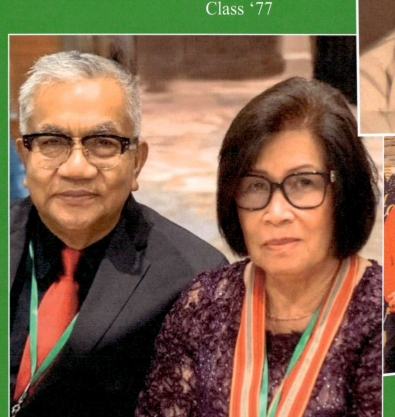

More Power to the BGHSNAA
and the BGHSNAA - Southern California

From **Ed and Fona Fornasdoro Family**

Congratulations from the Rudy & Aurea Liporada Clan

Aurea O. Liporada
Clinical Instructor
BGHSN
1975-1979

Thanks to the Organizers. We had a fabulous time!

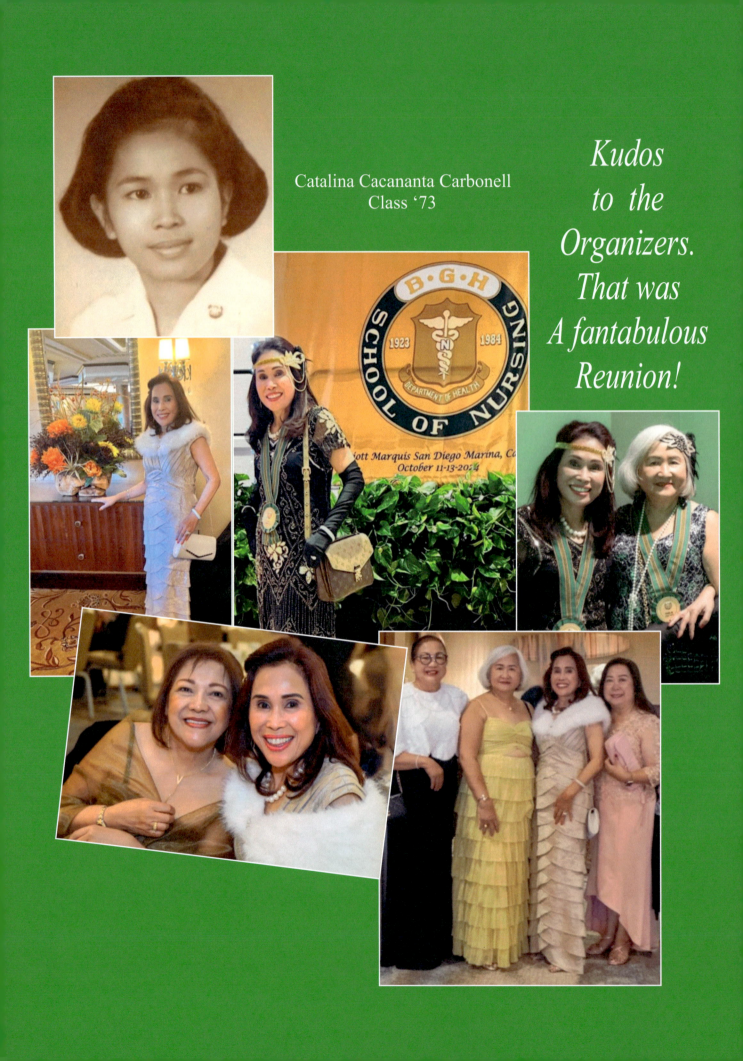

Catalina Cacananta Carbonell
Class '73

Kudos to the Organizers. That was A fantabulous Reunion!

Edna Rivera Gutierrez
Class '66

Thank you for a well organized Reunion! We had super fun reminiscing with former classmates and other alumni.

Arsenia Gonzales Smith
Class '77
with husband, Frank Smith

Thank You, Planners & Organizers for a well held Reunion! More power to the BGHSNAA Southern California!

What a Memorable Reunion!
Kudos to the Planners & Organizers!
More Power To the BGHSNAA Southern California

Marylyn Asprer-Lopez, Class '68, with husband, Dr. Ramon Lopez

Above Photo - Front l-r: Lorna Casarino Baird, Jane Tano Sali, Josie Mayo Ruiz; Back l-r: Nerisa Lagatao Tabora, Marylyn Asprer Lopez, Remy Rivera Go (class 1970)

Right Photo - Front l-r: Nerisa Lagatao Tabora, Josie Mayo Ruiz; Back l-r: Jane Tano Sali, Lolita Flores Shapiro, Marylyn Asprer Lopez

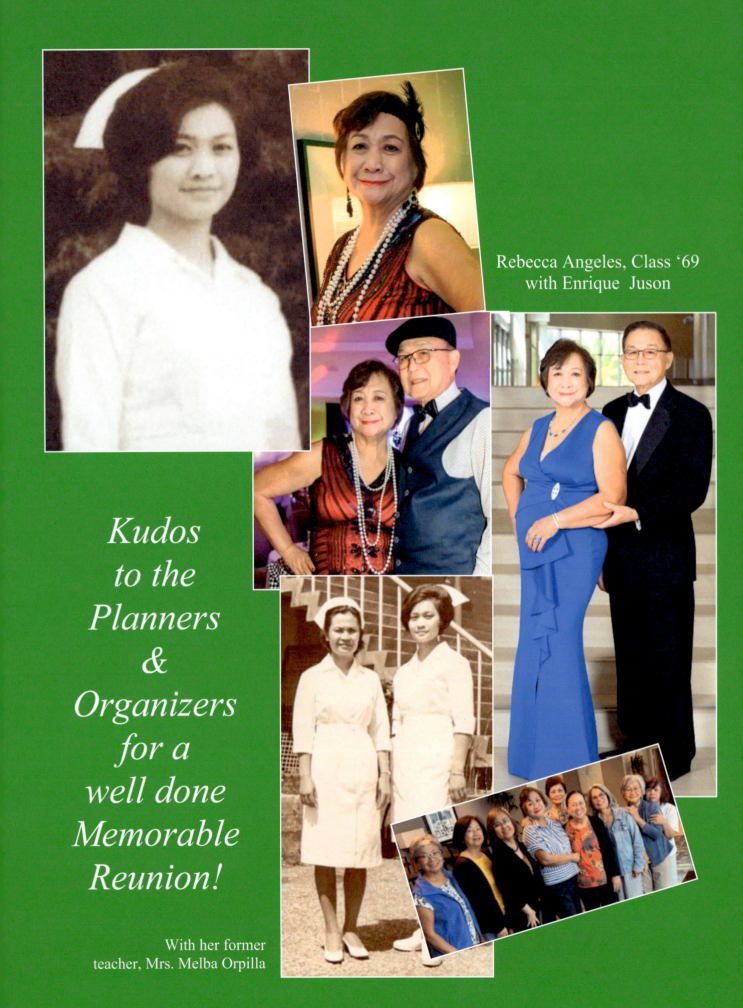

Rebecca Angeles, Class '69 with Enrique Juson

Kudos to the Planners & Organizers for a well done Memorable Reunion!

With her former teacher, Mrs. Melba Orpilla

Thank You!

Josie Ruiz, Class '68

I would have hated myself if I missed the 12th BGHSNAA International Reunion

Thank you for a Grand Reunion full of memories!

It was great being with former classmates and having fun with everyone!

Lorna Casarino Baird, '68

Tess Reyes Vidal,
Class '79,
With Romy Vidal

We had a blast at the Reunion. Kudos to the Planners & Organizers.

Cherished every moment, beautiful memories to remember forever!
Thank You.
Theresa Reyes Vidal '79

SoCal Charleston Dancers

Thank you for a wonderful Reunion!

Josie Raquedan Mejia
Class '74

It was fun, full of frolic, and memories to cherish. Kudos to the Planners And Organizers for a job well done!

Thank you!

Elvira Gonatice Bautista, Class '77, with husband, Art Bautista.

The reunion was a blast. Uniting with former classmates and schoolmates brought nostalgic memories. Euphoria Would be an understatement. Mabuhay BGHSNAA Southern California for planning and organizing the reunion.

Zenaida Bersamira,
Class '69,
with Tony Bersamira

Below is our Class '69
As Emerald celebrants.

Above is our family during our 50th wedding anniversary. At left, Tony and I are with our four grandchildren.

At left are our 'big sisters' of Class '67 during our school days. Up is our Class '69 during the picnic

*Thank You!
Kudos
to the Planners
and Organizers!*

Thelma Velbis,
Class '70,
with Andy Velbis

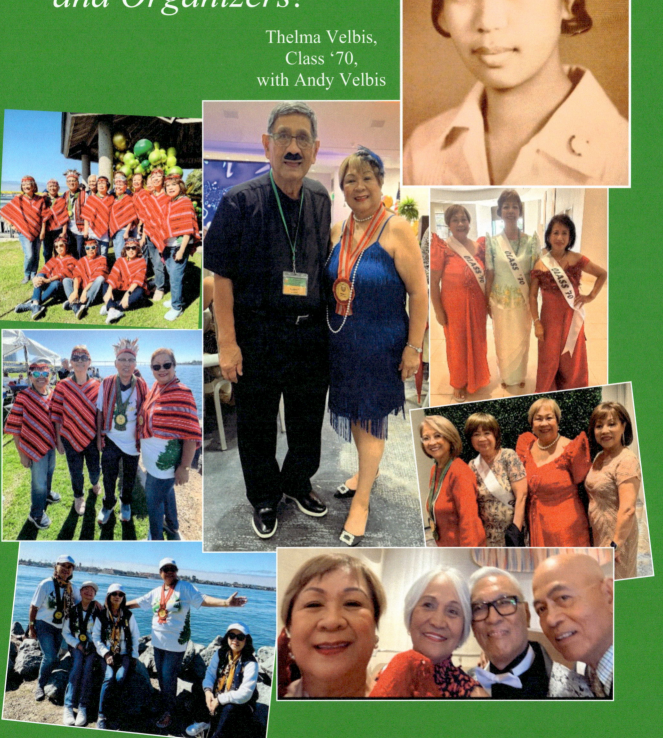

Collective diligence and perseverance paved the way to a successful reunion.

Connie Salaza-Asiong
Class '69

Skydiving is an intense, exhilarating experience that can be described as a mix of nerves, excitement, and sensory overload.

Thank You!

Zenaida de Guzman Razalan, Class '69, with Dr. Lee Razalan

Glad to have been part of the Planning And Organizing Committee!

Marivic Guidangen-Falatico
Valedictorian Class '82

At right Photo:
No less than
Principal Clotilda Leung Tom
pinned the Valedictorian Pin
on Maravic Guidangen
when she graduated
In 1982

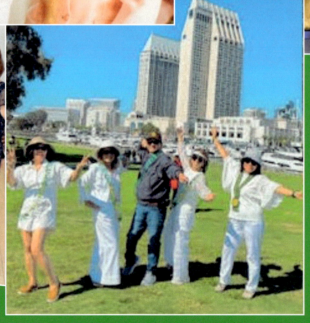

Among the 1980s graduates before BGHSN closed. Leftmost picture: L-R: Esther Jalandoni Padernal '82, Marieta Corpus Figueros '82, Noemi Sobrano Busacay '81, and Marivic Guidangen Falatico. Gentleman At left photo is Rolando G. Estigoy '83.

It was a memorable reunion! More Power to the BGHSNAA Southern California

"The Reunion was worth taking the trip from the Philippines."

Jane Galpo Pacalso
Class '76

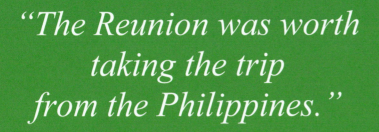

Glad to have been part of the Organizing Committee. The success was heartwarming!

Evilia Martin-Liganor
Class '59

Proud to have served with the Organizing Committee of a successful Reunion!

Melecia Edra Madrid, Class '67, with husband, Art Madrid

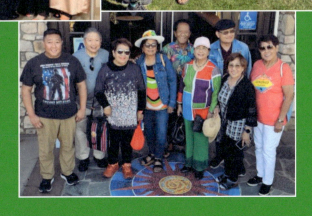

Rosita Serdenia-Cabula Cl'56

Olivia Bernardez-Salisi Cl'60

Marietta Herrera-Gaddi Cl'61

I want to be an RN, like MOM!

Thank you for a wonderful Reunion

From:
RN Children of RN Moms

12th BGHSNAA Grand International Reunion
October 11 - 13, 2024
Marriott Marquis San Diego, CA

Zenaida Flores-Bersamira, Class 1969

"When you have a dream, you've got to grab it, and never let go"

"Our 'hero' wears scrubs, and we call her 'MOM!' Now, we all wear scrubs! Don't miss the reunion, MOM!"

Christine B. Stone, RN

Allison B. Goedler, RN

Anthony James B, RN

Sailing through Time
The BGHSNAA 12th International Reunion That Never Was

The current 12th Baguio General Hospital School of Nursing Alumni Association International Reunion should have happened on June 25-27, 2021, at the renowned decommissioned ship, RMS Queen Mary, by Long Beach, California. As the ship, which was converted into a hotel, had its history, the theme for the reunion was "Sailing through Time."

In mid-2019, long before the reunion dates, preparations were in place, downpayments for the venue had been made, and everything was a go.

Then COVID happened.

Nonetheless, before then, former BGHSN CI Aurea Liporada, as a member of the organizing committee, wanted to feel the ambiance of the hotel. That way, during deliberations, she could stand on solid grounds or waters on her comments and suggestions. So, for

Above, the proposed Reunion Book cover for the supposed 12th reunion in 2021. At right, former CI Aurea Liporada by the replica of the MS Queen Mary.

her forthcoming birthday, we decided to spend a night on the ship.

Arriving in the late afternoon, I immediately felt the ship's immensity. The rays of the sinking sun, spread over the port side of the ship, forebode, to me, stories of antiquity, of historical significance. As we traversed the lobby to register, the ship started to breathe its former life to me – the rustic wooden panel walls, the artistry on the ceilings, the carpets, spoke of luxury; our room, was dotted with antique electric fans, and the like, even a toilet plunger – far from expectations of how it would serve that precipitated the downfall of the Axis power during WWII.

Suffice to say that, rivaling the Titanic, the RMS Queen Mary had its maiden voyage from Southampton, England to New York, the USA on May 1936. Previously tagged as Project 534, Queen Mary had it christened after her. It was England which provided the loan to the builder, Cunard, with the added demand that White Star, builder of the Titanic, be a partner builder.

Since then, the RMS Queen Mary became the most luxurious cruise ship at that time, crossing the Atlantic with the richest and most famous including entertainment personalities, politicians, and royalty.

Her glory days as luxurious were, however, postponed when WWII erupted in Europe in 1939. Winston Churchill requisitioned her to serve in the war arena. He called the ship the 'Gray Ghost' as it was painted gray to camouflage her especially in the dark. Transporting troops, she traversed the seas in a zig-zagging manner to throw German submarines and U-boats off their radars. Hitler had put a huge bounty on her for any submarine commander who could torpedo her. Unfortunately for the Germans, she could speed up to 40 knots while the enemy submarines could only do 20 knots. And even if she was fired upon, torpedoes could only be propelled to 20 knots. Zigzagging at enormous speed to ferry troops, Churchill claimed that she cut short the war by a year and a half.

The greatest war accomplishment of the RMS Queen Mary would be the transport of D-Day troops that won France back from the Germans. Another would be that, designed only to carry a little over 3,000, she transported 16,683 troops back home after the war – a record that had not been topped to this day.

Shortly after the war, the ship resumed her postponed luxurious glory days until economics took its toll. Within the sixties, air travel had become more popular than ocean voyages, which had become cumbersome. To cut losses, Cunard put the ship on a bidding sale. Long Beach in California won the bid for $3,450,000.00.

Thus, on December 9, 1967, the RMS Queen Mary docked at Sunny California to be transformed into the iconic hotel it is today.

Having said all these, the theme adopted by the BGHSNAA, "Sailing through Time," for their supposed 2021 reunion was most fitting for the function at the venue. The BGHSN closed its portals in 1984. In her 61 years, the school had produced 3,885 graduates who served and are serving, sharing their Tender Loving Care (TLC) to patients all over the world. Holding their reunion at the Queen Mary would have been an intertwining reminiscence of two glorious pasts. Like RMS Queen Mary's war service, the Nightingale's Light is forever lit. **RDLiporada**

The BGHSN Legacy

Professional Ethics
Core Values
Strength of Character
Compassion
Steadfast in Faith
Leadership
Focus
Determination

Connie Salaza Asiong
President, Class '69

Echoes of joy and excitement continue to ring true to those who graced us with their presence, even months after the incredibly successful 12th BGHSNAA International Grand Reunion.

It will be etched forever among the legacies of BGHSNAA.

This event was only made possible with the support of many people. We, therefore, extend our profound gratitude, specifically and generally, to the following: The officers of the BGHSNAA-SC, along with their families; the Planning Committees; the always gracious meeting hosts and their significant others and families, who unselfishly opened their homes to us; all of the participants of the 3-Day Program, especially the Class presentations and individuals who devoted their time and energy in preparing the event; and finally, the accommodating event planning staff of Marriott Marquis.

To those other countless people we couldn't include due to limited space, we offer our sincere gratitude for their support.

Class '69 Organizers through the years, we thank you!

It is great to see people who have been part of our lives! We impact each other, believe it or not! We have advanced physically in age, but God willing, with HIS continuous blessings of good health and prosperity, we will push on to look forward to more reunions despite all 'aches and pains.'

Thank you once again for your efforts! Take care, everyone,

First Row:
Jose & Dempta Baluda
Zeny & Tony Bersamira
Teresita Bugasto
Jane Cawis-Cabugao

Second Row:
Eleanor Daclan-Bayle
Jun & Elvie de Guzman-Flora
Lee & Zeny de Guzman-Razalan
Beatriz Espinosa-Santillan

Third Row:
Joe & Raquel Langit-Cabacungan
Vicky & Roland Lastimosa
Carmelita Lim-Aningalan
Carmen Macusi-Dingle

Fourth Row:
Eva Manlongat-Arnoldi
Letty & Rene Maniulit
Cynthia Marilla-Munar

Fifth Row:
Brenda Soriano-Villanueva
Malou Olarte-Visperas
Mila Rimando-Largo
Rebecca Ramos-Angeles

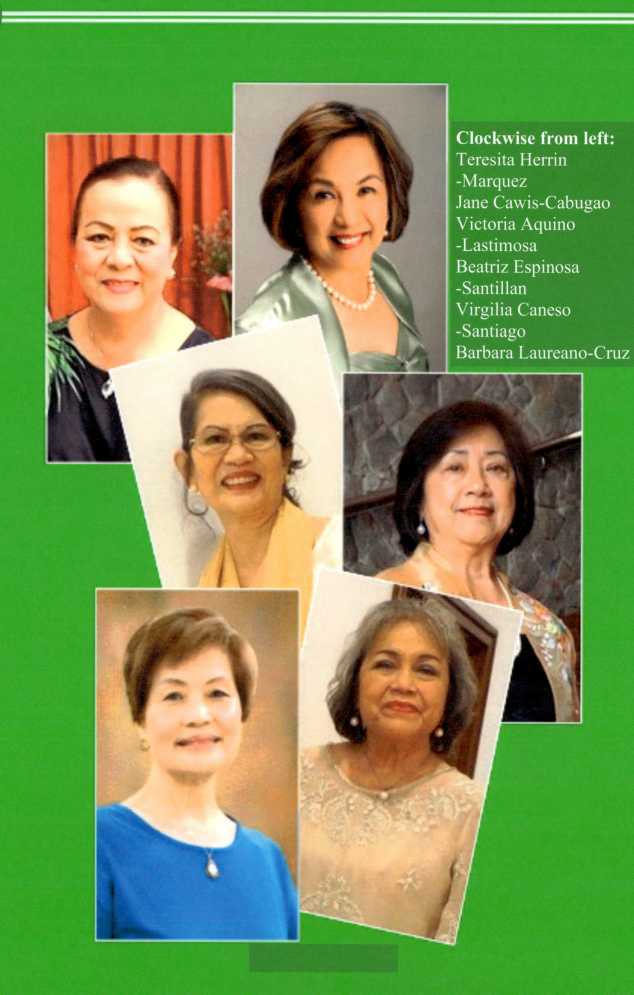

Clockwise from left:
Teresita Herrin-Marquez
Jane Cawis-Cabugao
Victoria Aquino-Lastimosa
Beatriz Espinosa-Santillan
Virgilia Caneso-Santiago
Barbara Laureano-Cruz

Clockwise from left:
Nida S. Cristobal
Jocelyn O. Luna
Leticia Siapno-Garg
Cipriana 'Tipin' Toledo-Alvarez
Cynthia Filomena Marilla-Munar
Zenaida Flores-Bersamira (Center)

From left, clockwise
Eleanor Daclan-Bayle
Jose P. Baluda
Lilia Villanueva-Sison
Brenda Soriano-Villanueva
Anita Quintos-Honrade
Feliciana Camat-Belvis

From leftmost-top, clockwise:
Alma Abellera -Vistro
Anelyn Dato-Penaflor
Bernadette Corpuz - Baxi
Loida Goyma-Aguilar
Carmelita Erangan -Tayag
Teresita A. Bugasto

Top (l-r)
Arcadio Quitos, Jr.
Carmelita Eugenio-Labagday
Elizabeth Amoyen-Barros
Middle (l-r)
Raquel Langit-Cabacungan
Gloria Baterina
Letty Tomas-Maniulit
Cynthia A. Guinto
Bottom (l-r)
Brenda Magno-Cue
Dalisay Leoncio-Ting
Ligaya Palaganas-Fontanilla
Ditas M. Burdios

Top (l-r): Eleazar Rullan, Norma Tuliao-La Putt, Alicia Barnachea-Meana, Sylvia Valdez- Bautista
Middle (l-r): Resurreccion Gozon-Sanchez, Zenaida de Luna-Plata, Rosa Backong-Padong, Mary Lou Olarte-Visperas
Bottom: (l-r): Evangeline Carillo-Gumnad, Josephine Dimalanta-Pangilinan, Elvie de Guzman-Flora, Luis Jack Laurico

Congratulations
And more Power
To the Organizers
Of this 12th BGHSNAA
International Reunion!

Mila Rimando-Largo

Carmen Macusi-Dingle

Cheers to 55 years of cherished friendships, endless laughter, and unwavering companionships! As we celebrate our emerald anniversary, let's honor the enduring bond that has fortified us through the years. Sending love to all my wonderful classmates!

After nursing school, we each took our path but carried a piece of each other. Our shared experiences shaped us into compassionate and capable nurses. In retirement, let's continue to support and inspire each other. May God bless our journeys. Happy 55th year, batch 1969!

Beatrice V. Olais

Zenaida De Guzman -Razalan

From our family, greetings and warmest welcome to all my BGHSN co-alumni and guests. Thank you for coming and sharing these valuable days with us. Let's laugh together one more time, smile brightly with each other one more time, and hug each other one more time. Together let's add more beautiful and precious remembrances to our bank of BGHSN memories.

Children
Lee J
Zendy
Leah
Eunice

Grandchildren
Alex
Holden
Olivia
Allysa
William
Elorah
Reza

Rebecca Ramos-Angeles

"Happy 55th anniversary of graduating from BGHSN to Grandma Rebecca. She has shown us that love only deepens with time. We hope her special day is as extraordinary as her love for each of us. Congratulations to the esteemed Class of 1969."

Eva Manlongat-Arnoldi

Chelsea

Francis

Tori

Coca

"Join us in celebrating Grandma Eva's remarkable achievement of 55 years since graduating from BGHSN. Her enduring love is an inspiration to us all. Let's make her special day extraordinary as her love for each of us. Congratulations to the esteemed Class of 1969 for their outstanding accomplishments."

To our Shining Star Mama Femmie, Congratulations on achieving your status as a 55th-year Jubiliarian with the prestigious BGHSN Class of 1969!!! From your children and grandchildren who love you to the moon and back!

Eufemia Ducusin-Bersamin

Camille and Yale Sommer and their children (Marshall, Wyatt, and Charlotte); Veronica and Junmo Jo and their kids (Brandon and Vanellope); Rene JR Bersamira and Alayne with their children, Quinn and baby Raphael (still in the womb).

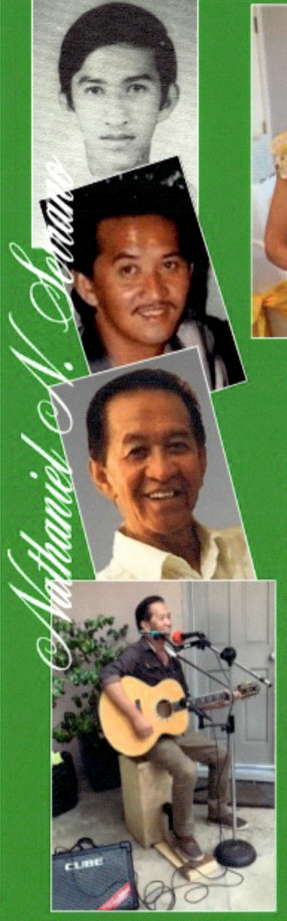

Paul and Monette
N. Serrano - Nordson

Remembering brother Nathaniel N. Serrano And classmates

Monette N. Serrano-Nordson and her husband Paul Nordson dedicate this page to the memory of her brother Nathaniel N. Serrano and other departed members of the Class of 1969.

Over the years, we sometimes hear the unwelcome news of a classmate's passing. Reading or learning about their cause of death often makes us pause in disbelief and wonder: "how could this have happened?"

In life, we go through peaks and valleys, successes and failures, and many wins and losses. Life presents contrasting experiences, akin to the changing seasons. Ecclesiastes 3:2-8 illustrates this, assuring that everything has its time, and God makes everything beautiful in its own time (Ecclesiastes 3:11).

Our dearly departed classmates

Egonia V. Albarillo-Bonoan	Nora Doriano-Aberin
Bernardina C. Arquero-Baterina	Arsenio M. Dulos
Virginia C. Balinong	Zenaida Ganuelas-Grepo
Norma Banez-Zaide	Rogelio V. Orlina
Clementina Bernardo-Toquero	Maria T. Pepe
Paz Carantes-Tamayo	Nathaniel N. Serrano
Grace Dangatan	Elizabeth Velasco-Palma

We pray for the repose of their souls!

Class '69 The Last BGHSN Dormitory Residents

We, the Class of 1969, proudly stood as the last group of nursing students to inhabit the Nurses' Dorm for a full 3 years (1966-1969). Despite its challenges, the experience undeniably fostered deep unity among us. Now, in our retirement from nursing, every opportunity to visit classmates becomes a cherished chance to come together, share stories, and celebrate the lasting bond we formed during our time in the Nurses' Dorm.

Class '69 Sydney, Australia Escapade
Feb. 21 - Mar. 2 2019

How fortunate we were to tour the most scenic places of Sydney, Australia, in the company of the most gracious of hosts, Dr. Joe, Raquel (Langit), and their daughter, Michelle Cabacungan!

A big group of 37 (25 members belonging to Class 69 plus two from Class 68) stayed in Sydney for ten days. Swissotel (a five-star hotel) was a big PLUS! It was conveniently located in downtown area with all the amenities and shopping centers around for us from the USA and the Philippines.

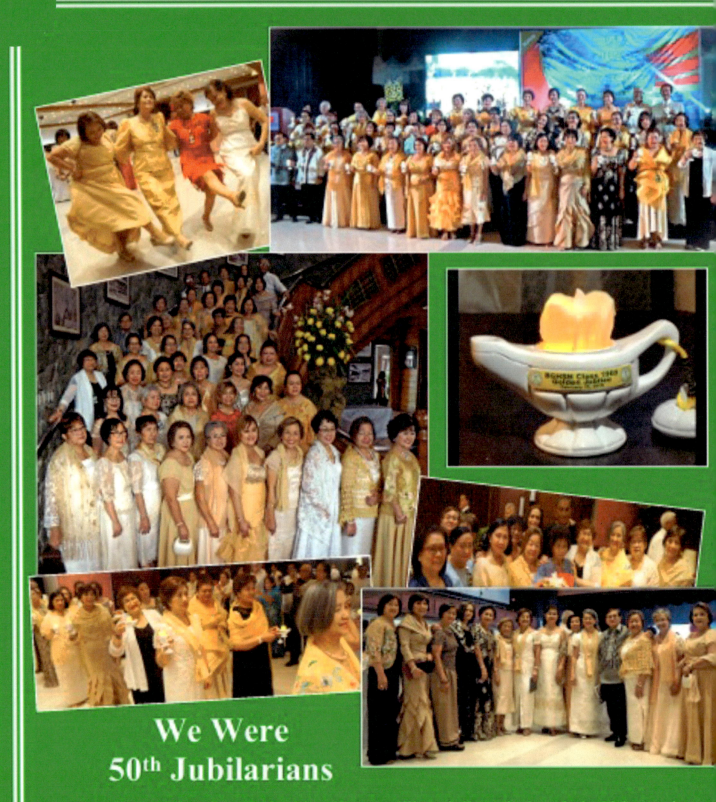

We Were 50th Jubilarians

Dressed in their best and looking like a million dollars during their 50th Anniversa Jubilee, the Class of 1969 assembled for a truly memorable and heartfelt 3-Day reunion Camp John Hay, Baguio City, Philippines. The vast majority of the attendees were fr the United States of America. We take this opportunity to thank the Class of 1979 for b sponsoring and organizing this wonderful event.

FROM THE EMERALD JUBILARIANS- CLASS OF 1969

It was wonderful to catch up with all the BGHSN Alumni. This reunion provided a great opportunity to reconnect with everyone from both upper and lower classes, along with their families. This isn't a farewell but rather a 'see you next time' at the next BGHSN reunion, which we hope will be soon. The three days and nights we spent together were not enough to socialize with everyone we knew or to get to know all the new friends we made. It truly felt like a 'grand' family reunion. What a beautiful gathering to remember!

Thank you to everyone who attended, and more power to the Southern California group for organizing the event. Let's continue to foster this wonderful camaraderie and keep the spirit of BGHSN alive in our hearts and minds forever. Thank you, Dr. Teodoro Arvisu, and all the mentors!

Baguio General Hospita

Alma A. Abellera- Vistro
Chula Vista, CA, USA
Conchita W. Alban-Valdez
New York, USA
Egonia V. Albarillo-Bonoan (+)
Elizabeth G. Amoyen-Barros
San Francisco, CA, USA
Cynthia F. Aquino- Guinto
Old Bridge, NJ, USA
Victoria E. Aquino- Lastimosa
Renton, WA, USA
Bernardina C. Arquero-Baterina (+)
Connie S. Asiong
Panorama City, CA, USA
Rosa B. Backong- Padong
Baguio City, PI
Ellen A. Bahingawan
Montreal, Quebec, Canada
Virginia C. Balinong (+)
Jose P. Baluda
Baguio City, PI
Noma B. Banez- Zaide (+)
Anita Baptista
Hawaii, USA
Alicia Barnachea- Meana
Baguio City, PI
Gloria F. Baterina
Houston, TX, USA
Clementina Bernardo-Toquero (+)
Teresita A. Bugasto
Chicago, Illinois, USA
Miriam A. Buted-de Guzman
Kingsport, TN, USA
Ruben L. Calpito
Quebec, Canada
Feliciana C. Camat- Belvis
Edmonton, Alberta, Canada
Ofelia O. Camat-Agbulos
Edmonton, Alberta, Canada
Amorita R. Caoile
New York, USA

Virgilia C. Caneso- Santiago
San Diego, CA, USA
Paz L. Carantes-Tamayo (+)
Evangeline L. Carillo-Gumnad
Baguio City, PI
Jane L. Cawis- Cabugao
Vallejo, CA, USA
Bernadette T. Corpuz-Baxi
Vallejo, CA, USA
Bienvenida S. Cristobal
Walnut, CA, USA
Eleanor Daclan-Bayle
Vallejo, CA, USA
Grace Dangatan (+)
Anelyn O. Dato-Penaflor
San Jose, CA, USA
Josephine Dimalanta-Pangilinan
Baguio City, PI
Nora B. Doriano- Aberin (+)
Eufemia Ducusin-Bersamin
Hixson, Tennessee
Arsenio M. Dulos (+)
Carmelita Erangan-Tayag
Bowie, Maryland, USA
Beatrice V. Espinosa- Santillan
Las Vegas, NV, USA
Evangeline V. Esquejo- Mogan
Escondido, CA, USA
Carmelita E. Eugenio-Labagday
Quezon, City, PI
Oscar R. Farnacio
Emerson, NJ, USA
Nina F. Feria- Mangosing
Chula Vista, CA
Zenaida M. Flores- Bersamira
Escondido, CA, USA
Zenaida L. Ganuelas-Grepo (+)
Elnora P. Garcia-Hoganas
Chesapeake Bay, VA, USA
Bernardita Gonzales

School of Nursing Class '69

Loyda G. Goyma-Aguilar
San Jose, CA, USA
Resureccion Gozon-Sanchez
Bulacan, PI
Elvira Z. de Guzman-Flora
Baguio City, PI
Zenaida S. de Guzman-Razalan
Rancho Palos Verdes, CA, USA
Teresita D. Herrin-Marquez
Peoria, AZ, USA
Alicia I. Ibanez
Palmdale, CA, USA
Jean P. Julian-Ruiz
Michigan, USA
Martha A. Kebasen-Bartolomei
Switzerland
Raquel L. Langit-Cabacungan
Sydney, Australia
Barbara R. Laureano-Cruz
Quezon City, PI
Luis Jack S. Laurico
San Fernando, La Union, PI
Dalisay R. Leoncio-Ting
Calgary, Alberta, Canada
Carmelita S. Lim-Aningalan
Bellerose, NY, USA
Jocelyn O. Luna
Albany, CA, USA
Zenaida S. de Luna-Plata
Angeles City, Pampanga, PI
Carmen G. Macusi-Dingle
Roseville, CA
Zenaida B. Maglanoc
Yonkers, NY, USA
Brenda A. Magno- Cue
Burlingame, CA
Eva Manlongat- Arnoldi
Chino, CA
Cynthia S. Marilla-Munar
Jersey City, NJ, USA
Ditas Montemayor- Burdios
Union City, CA, USA
Rosalinda Naoe- Sagles
New York, USA

Beatrice V. Olais
Van Nuys, CA, USA
MaryLou Olarte- Visperas
Quezon City, PI
Rogelio V. Orlina (+)
Estrella O. Pacheco-Bautista
Sewell, NJ, USA
Fe G. Padre- Viado
El Paso, TX, USA
Ligaya Palaganas - Fontanilla
La Crescenta, CA, USA
Maria T. Pepe (+)
Arcadio S. Quitos, Jr.
Leesburg, Florida, USA
Anita Quintos- Honrade
San Jose, CA
Rebecca E. Ramos-Angeles
Piscataway, New Jersey, USA
Milagros Rimando-Largo
Vallejo, CA, USA
Eleazar M. Rullan
La Union, PI
Nathaniel N. Serrano (+)
Leticia Siapno-Garg
Austin, Texas, USA
Brenda A. Soriano-Villanueva
Leonardtown, Maryland, USA
Elizabeth M. Soriano- Padilla
Los Angeles, CA, USA
Leticia N. Tomas- Maniulit
Ewa Beach, Hawaii, USA
Cipriana Toledo- Alvarez
Cherry Hills, New Jersey, USA
Norma Tuliao- La Putt
Pasig City, PI
Edmour Valdez
Montreal, Quebec, Canada
Sylvia Valdez- Bautista
Baguio City, PI
Elizabeth Velasco- Palma (+)
Teresita de Venecia- Centeno
Austin, Texas, USA
Lilia Villanueva- Sison
Leonardtown, Maryland, USA

Vignettes of BGHSN History

BGH nursing school building inaugurated today

Puyat is guest speaker at morning ceremonies

BAGUIO CITY, Oct. 27 —(CNS)— Senator Gil Puyat, NP candidate for Vice President, will be the guest speaker 9:30 this morning at a program in connection with the formal inauguration of the new Baguio General Hospital school of nursing building.

Dedicated to the education of Filipino nurses that they may elevate the standard of the profession in serving ailing humanity, the BGHSN edifice is believed the first school building solely for nurses outside of Manila.

Mrs. Salud O. Mitra, wife of Rep. Ramon P. Mitra, will cut the ceremonial ribbon during the inauguration. She will be assisted by Mrs. Flora Crosby, vice chairman, BGH advisory board and Dr. Hector T. Lopez, officer-in-charge. The blessing of the building will be officiated by Fr. Alberto Van Pelt, hospital chaplain, after which the singing of the National Anthem led by Mrs. Leonora V. Aguilar, nursing arts instructor will formally open the inaugural program. Dr. Hector Lopez is master of ceremonies.

The guests speaker will be introduced by Mayor Luis L. Lardizabal, following a word of welcome by Fernando Bautista, president of the BGH advisory board.—jcr

DR. JUSTO R. ROSALES
Chief, BGH

DR. HECTOR T. LOPEZ
Officer in charge-BGH

MRS. GAVINA L. CRUZ
Administrative officer, BGH

IRENE F. FRANCIA
Chief Nurse & Actg. Supt.

MRS. CLOTHILDA L. TOM
Principal

MRS. ALMA A. PAYNOR
Assistant Principal

Modern BGH School of Nursing Building—An architect's drawing of the P121-thousand Baguio General Hospital school of nursing building to be inaugurated today (Oct. 27) with Senator Gil Puyat as guest of honor. Situated on one-hectare grounds adjoining the BGH Nurses Home, this two-story building contains two spacious classrooms, a library, faculty, laboratory-rooms and offices of the principal and assistant principal, besides a 1,000 seating capacity auditorium on the first floor. The basement provides living quarters for male nursing students.—jcr

Baguio General Hospital Advisory Board. Shown above are members of the BGH Advisory Board. Front row, left to right: Miss Irene Francia, Mrs. Fannie Contemprate, Mrs. Betty Ploesser, Fernando Bautista, chairman of the board; Mrs. Flora Crosby, vice chairman; Mrs. Virginia Paraan, secretary; Mrs. Cleotilda Tom. Second row: Mrs. Mary Kneebone; Mrs. Gorgonia Ladines, Mrs. Felicidad Perez, Dr. Josefina Gorospe, Mrs. Teodora M. Flores, treasurer; Mrs. Mary Gorospe and Julian Reyes. Back row: Leopoldo Peñera, Lam Far, Marcial Zaguirre, Dr. Antonio H. Adorable, Dr. Hector Lopez, Ossie Hamada, Ricardo A. Paraan and Teofilo Estigoy. Not in the picture: Mrs. Libertad Quetulio, Eugene P. Pucay, Eusebio Botengan and Dr. Carlos G. Santiago, Jr. (Photo by Johnny Gonzales).

Messages

I extend warmest greetings to the faculty members and staff of the Baguio General Hospital School of Nursing on the inauguration of their new school building.

This edifice is the answer to the long-felt need for comfortable rooms for holding classes of student nurses in this region. Classroom environment plays an important role in facilitating and improving student learning. Besides adding beauty to the place, this schoolbuilding should afford adequate instructional facilities for training ambitious young men and women desiring to pursue nursing as a career.

I wish success to the Baguio General Hospital School of Nursing whose graduates will in time help raise health standards in the rural areas of the Mountain Province in line with the health progarm of our government.

CARLOS P. GARCIA
President

I am highly gratified to learn of the inauguration of the new school building of the Baguio General Hospital School of Nursing.

With the improved facilities and expanded accommodations of this institution, I hope the Baguio General Hospital School of Nursing will successfully continue it's chosen mission of producing competent and dedicated nurses who shall devote their lives to the caring of the sick.

To the staff of the Baguio General Hospital and to all those who have contributed to the realization of this project my sincere congratulations!

DIOSDADO MACAPAGAL
Vice President

1923 and Memories

On this our School's Diamond Jubilee
we look into the time machine and
what do we see?

The year is 1923
The Baguio Hospital School of Nursing as
conceived by men of vision is born

Through all these years,
the school has served well and with distinction
its constituents especially the poor and the minorities.

Soon the portals of the school will close,
perhaps forever

Those who feel abandoned and betrayed should remember
that many from all walks of life, and stations in life, tried to
stay the sentence on an institution

On this Diamond Jubilee, somehow we realize
our school, unlike diamonds, is not forever

First it was a dream, then an institution
that served long and well

Soon it will be just a memory, perhaps even a legend.

Written by
Aurora P. Tenefrancia, RN, ED.D
Class 1955 - December 16-17, 1983
BGHMC-DECMMC Diamond Jubilee

From Sanatorium to Medical Center
From School to Legend

A lot has happened since the beginning of the hospital, from a crude civil sanatorium to the medical center that it is today. It has a history of events, buildings, and people. It also has a story of several successes and achievements of heartaches and failures. For like any story, there is the good and the bad. To be sure, some are earnestly striving for nothing less than perfection. Whether they will be able to attain this ideal or not, we salute them for at least trying.

A far-reaching event that will take place in the near future is the phasing out of the BGH School of Nursing. The Alumni Association, and the Faculty are working hard for its retention. In fact, they are working on a change of curriculum from Graduate Nurse to Bachelor of Science in Nursing.

Resolutions for the retention of the school and if possible, a change of curriculum from Graduate Nurse to Bachelor of Science in Nursing from political and professional organizations, petitions signed by the alumni, concerned citizens, civic and professional organizations, educational and religious institutions here and abroad as well as newspaper clippings were furnished to the Minister of Health (MOH) Jesus Azurin, the Batasang Pambansa, and President Ferdinand E. Marcos. Even a petition to President Marcos signed by all the Assemblymen of Region I, was followed up by Minister Jose D. Aspiras.

The School of Nursing has become an 'Institution' in itself. Through the years, the good work and the great potential for service and education of the school are well known. Despite all these, it seems the school may not have many more years to serve.

So, from dream to reality, the Baguio General Hospital School of Nursing will soon be part of history. But to its proud alumni, a total of 3,885, and for those who believe and fought for what it stands for, the School of Nursing of the BH, the BGHMC, and finally, DECMMC will forever be a legend. At this point, the lines from Camelot somehow seem poignantly relevant.

> "Let it not be forgotten
> There once was a spot
> On one brief shining moment
> That was known as Camelot."

Thank you, all faculty, staff, adminstrators, supporters, and Dr. Teodoro C. Arvisu.

By Aurora Pe-Benito Tenefrancia
BGHSN Class 1955

Remembering the Founder and the Mentors

Dr. Teodoro C Arvisu
Founder - BGHSN
In 1922

Clotilda Leung Tom
CI - 1944

Alma Aguirre-Paynor
CI - 1945

Irene R. Francia
UP-PGH Alumna

Aurora Pe Benito Tenefrancia
CI - 1955

Dr. Teodoro C. Arvisu established the Baguio Hospital School of Nursing (BGHSN) in 1922. Congress approved the school's creation that same year. Dr. Arvisu then was serving as the second chief of the Baguio Hospital from 1919 to 1936. The first chief nurse was Miss Maria B. Defensor.

"To its proud alumni, the Baguio General Hospital School of Nursing will forever be a legend"

With Gratitude, Thank You!

The impetus to establish the BGHSN roots from the founding of the Baguio General Hospital itself. In 1915, the supervision of the hospital was turned over to the Bureau of Health with Dr. Vincent as the last American chief of hospital. The first Filipino director who was appointed in that same year was Dr. Silverio Garcia. He was succeeded by Dr. Marcelino Azucano and Dr. Jose Avellana Basa. It was after then, when Dr. Teodoro Arvisu became Chief, that he, subsequently, established the BGHSN in 1922.

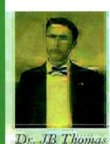

The hospital started as Baguio Sanatorium in February 3, 1902 pioneered by Dr. Eugene Stafford, captain of the staff of General Arthur MacArthur in the 1900's.

The hospital begun as a convalescent sanatorium in a small grass roofed building at the former side of Pines hotel or the present exact location of Shoemart (SM) today. Dr. Stafford brought with him a nurse, a cook, and an assistant.

Originally, it began as an 8-bed sanatorium and on March 25, 1902, the construction of a 15-bed capacity hospital consisting of six 3-room cottages was built. It was manned by American physicians, army nurse, and hospital corpsmen. Dr. JB Thomas was the first chief of hospital back then.

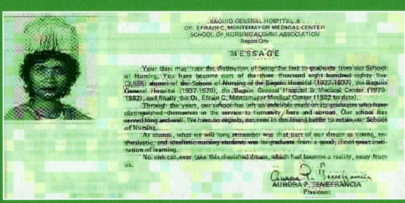

Since its establishment in 1922 to its closure in 1984, the BGHSN had graduated 3,885 student nurses who served and are still serving far and wide everywhere, even in far-flung corners of the world. Early graduates also served under fire and bombings during World War II. A number served in war fronts including with the Operation Brotherhood during the Vietnam War. Many were frontliners with a number giving the ultimate sacrifice during COVID era. In all these nursing endeavors, they were ready, theoretically and practically equipped, as honed by able administrators and faculty members.

Top: BGHSNAA President and Supervising Nurse Instructor Aurora P. Tenefrancia's address to the last batch of graduates in 1984.
Right and below: Faculty members during the 1960's, 1970's, and 1980's.

We trudged up and down those steps, leading us to our society's notches of service. Thank you very much, Baguio General Hospital School of Nursing.

Class of 1940's senior nursing students excursion to Bunuan Beach with some BGH medical and nursing staff.

Above: The class of 1941 with Ms. Irene Francia, Chief Nurse, BGH, and Principal of the School of Nursing (seated in the middle second row). To her right is Concepcion Mamaril-Lesaca (Class Valedictorian and Board of Nursing Exam Topnotcher.)

Right: The First BGHSNAA Grand International Reunion was held in Oakbrook, Illinois, July 17-19, 1992. Holding the BGHSNAA banner proudly from L-R: Cristina Lacsamana-Chan (Cl'42). Juanita Lamug-Cadsawan (Cl'58), Alma Aguirre-Paynor (Cl'45), Corazon Agor (CL' 58) and Melba Rillera-Orpilla (Cl'45).

Right: BGHSN Alumni from different classes, each wearing tops and caps of shades and colors. What a joyful sight to see, the interplay of colors! It is like seeing 'The Colorful Olympic Rings - Symbol of the Olympic Movement!" This was held during the BGHSNAA 11th International Grand Alumni Homecoming picnic at the Camp John Hay Bell Garden in Feb 17, 2019. This was hosted by the Class of 1979.

Participating in the celebration of the 6th Anniversary of the Commonwealth—November 15, 1941.

A month after the photo above was taken, on December 8, 1941, Japan launched an attack on the Philippines, ten hours after their attack on Pearl Harbor. The student nurses above were thrown into service amidst bombing in the duration of the war endangering also their lives.

Encircled in the picture is Belen Cristobal-Frias, an aunt of Nida Cristobal of Class '69 and a former BGHSN instructor. "I remember her sharing stories about how, right after graduation, they were 'mandated' to report to the hospital due to war casualties. It only dawned on me when I looked closely at the photo using a magnifying lens and I recognized her," Cristobal said.

The Japanese forces seized the hospital for their own use on 1944 and the hospital staff transferred to the Saint Louis High School building located behind the Baguio Cathedral to continue to serve patients despite the bombings by the advancing American forces.

At left, three bombs fell by the right wing of the hospital, one hit and two near misses. Craters were 20 x 12 feet.

Public health nursing by plane? just posing for a souvenir in Loakan Airport with a dream that someday the plane will take them abroad.

Rosita Serdenia-Cabula
of Class 1956
could have been
in the parade.

Awarded the most colorful and orderly group during the Independence Day Parade in 1956.

The Last Ditch Petition to Save Baguio General Hospital School of Nursing

Minister Jesus Azurin, during a national meeting of Regional Health Directors, Provincial Health Officers, Chief of Hospitals and the Medical Staff and Department Heads of BGHMMC, was caught by surprise by the faculty and students of the School of Nursing when they marched in bearing placards, appealing for nurses and other members of the health team including the retention of the School of Nursing for the minorities and the poor.

Mrs. Aurora P. Tenefrancia presented the sentiments of the group during the Open Forum, December 12, 1983, 12:30 p.m.

The Evolution of the Baguio General Hospital and Medical Center

Baguio Sanatorium

From a Sanatorium to expansion

Through war destruction, redevelopment and modernization; to what it is now at present.

- Where BGHSN used to be, now administration offices; surrounding buildings are for Trauma and Heart centers
- OPD, Rehab, Dental, Opthalmology, Lab, Pysche, Drug Rehab
- Billing, Registration, EENT, Endoscopy, Chapel, Newborn clinic
- Triage, Surgery, ICU, Ortho, Blood Bank, Central supply
- Emergency, general internal medicine, pediatric care, diagnostic imaging, Infectious diseases, Poisoning, Burns
- Patient Wards
- BGH Entrance

BGHSN Schoool Song

From yonder mountains full of pines,
Beneath the skies of radiant beauty,
Our school beloved proudly shines
To me the paragon of purity
Climbing morning glory thy path adorn
Made fresh and green by sun-kissed dew
The floating mist where clouds are born
Keep crowning over its stalwart yew.

Along the slopes of grasses green
Across the paths that birds may tread
Stands young and fragile ever been
The land of choice that is thy bed
We love the BGH as ever
We praise thee always and forever
Though foreign lands our steps may go
In spirit high we cling to you.

BGHSN Alma Mater Song

We venture out along the highlands
Sheltered thick with hills and mountains
Under shades our ALMA MATER stands
Embered true from stream to fountains
Far away our trods may wander stray
Thy love and care shall ever taunt
My prudent heart where'er it may
Despair and mirth, thy flame shall haunt

Our service kind and true shall give
To care for those that shall be healed
That illness cured and they may live
To see the light, the Lord hath sealed
Thy poignant mem'ries we'll behold
Thy standard we shall carry high
Thy banner to the top uphold
Thy name shall stand in ev'ry sigh.

CHORUS

BGH, so dear and true to me
When'er the days may seem so blue
Lift then our hearts that we may see
Oh! ALMA MATER the dawn in you.

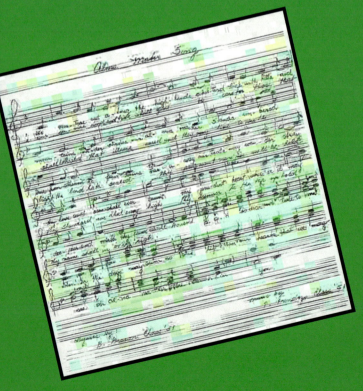

How the ReminiscenceS evolved

The ReminiscenceS book was produced with the convergence of a staff who loves to capture, gather, and preserve telling moments, memories that are kept over the passage of time. Nida Cristobal, a former graduate and instructor of the Baguio General Hospital Nursing School, is a history buff. She has found the book as a chest of facts about the hospital, the school, and her former students and colleagues. Although the facts may not be that complete, ReminiscenceS provide a glimpse of a historical project that may yet unfold.

Rudy D. Liporada's involvement in the book roots from his affinity with the school by virtue of being married to Aurea Liporada, who was also a former instructor in the school. He had offered to use his experiences since his high-school days in the production of print media. He has authored several books; been an editor of ethnic newspapers; taught feature writing, photography, and advertising in Zambia, Africa; and, as a writer for on-line newspapers and magazines, he maintains 'As the Bamboos Sway' as his column.

Fona Fornasdoro was the chairperson of the Souvenir Book for the 12th Grand Hospital School of Nursing Alumni Association International Grand Reunion. Together, with her husband, Ed Fornasdoro, they facilitated the gathering of vital nputs into ReminiscenceS.

Roy 'Saleng ken Marapait' Reclosado took valuable pictures incorporated into the Book. He also coordinated with Bert Magsino to produce video clips of the functions from which Cristobal patiently screen shot photos also used in the Book.

Melody Tubis, caretaker of the Cristobals in their Baguio City ancestral home, dug into the personal archives of the Cristobals to add necessary pictures and facts into the Book. Magda Dawowong, the librarian of the Baguio General Hospital, also was the conduit in providing materials for the history, relevant personalities, and related facts about the hospital.

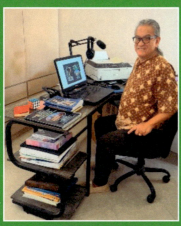

Nida Cristobal, above, says that "The Book 'ReminiscenceS caused many sleepless nights, but it was the source of so much joy and treasured memories." At right, Rudy Liporada just wants to put it on record that the layout of the Book was finished in Baja, Mexico.

Albeit, Amazon describes the Book as: The book, ReminiscenceS, is a novelty. Hardbound to last, it is a treasury chest book of memories of the 12th Baguio General Hospital School of Nursing Alumni Association International Grand Reunion held in Oct. 11-13, 2024, in San Diego, California. Packed with over 200 pages of images are the ringing voices of former students of the School as they celebrated their gathering from all over the world to reminisce their youthful years to become professional nurses, swapping stories of how they navigated their journeys to success in their niches in their service to humanity. The intensity of their reminiscences was accented with sounds of roaring twenties and oldies music to which they gyrated and swayed to their hearts' content. Their sweet farewells after were wishes of longing for the next gathering. From its inauguration in 1923 to its closing in 1984, the school had 3,885 graduates march out from her portals.

"ReminiscenceS" as title of the Book was adopted by the staff after Nora Salvatoriello called out that a name change was necessary in place of the original title, which, although it could also mean what we meant, it connotes more what happens after disasters and catastrophes.

We wanted the Happy Moments!

Above, l-r: Roy Reclosado and Bert Magsino. At Right: Ed and Fona Fornasdoro. Below, l-r: Melody Tubis and Magdalena Dawowong,

Nida Cristobal invited her former co-instructors to help proofread the sample ReminiscenceS book. At her right is Chit Boquiren and at her left are Liway Luczon and Aurea Liporada. The proof session made their Christmas lunch at the Luczons most enjoyable. **ABphoto**

We also acknowledge and thank the following for helping in captioning the pictures with the names of the attendees and unearthing the graduation pictures of the same:
Nida Cristobal, Fona Fornasdoro, Georgina Aquino-Cadalin, Nancy Villa, Aurora Baduria, Naty Savellano, Jane Bullecer, Crisabel Ramos, Marivic Guidangen Falatico, Nellie Dawana Reyes, and Edna Rivera Gutierrez.

We also apologize for any errors of commission and omission we may have made. They were not done with malicious intentions. -ReminiscenceS Staff-

A *Toast* for a grateful Sentiment

"I commend the entire committee for organizing such a wonderful grand reunion. Thank you for your hard work and dedication. I know you've spent years preparing and ensuring that this event met the goals of a meaningful reunion. I join my classmates (Class 1970) and many others in applauding your efforts. Those who participated feel blessed to have had another opportunity to reconnect with old friends and acquaintances. We hope to all gather again in another four years for another memorable reunion."

Tom Madayag
Valedictorian Class '70

At the BGHSNAA - Southern California Planners and Organizers reunion recap meeting Dec. 1, 2024 courtesy of hosts Romy & Tess Vidal

Fona, Ed, Mary, Seny, Zeny

Herman, Pinky, Fortune, Art, Rheza

"A reunion made of beautiful memories that will last a lifetime!"
-Nida Cristobal-

"Proud to be a part of this group."
-Josie Ruiz-

Zendy, Josie, Mila, Marlena,

"I met so many new friends and have many memories to keep."
-Zendy Razalan-

Connie, Irma, Thelma, Zeny, Evilia

Thanks for everyone's support in making the reunion a success!
-Cris Ramos-

Tess, Romy, Cris, Au, Rudy

"We did very good" - Almost everyone in varying words.-

Josie, Gina, Lorna, Robert

"We brought the most attendees. We will be more next time."
-Gina Cadalin-

Not able to attend:

Carrie Ramos
Mildred Hizon
Nellie dela Pena
Merle Arceo
Myrna Aganos
Gloria Duty
Wilfred Ballesil
Eva Mamaril
Naty Savellano
Jovet Jose
Mel Madrid
Susie Macayan
Helen Camero
Brenda Leal

Photos by Saleng Ken Marapait

Heads Up...

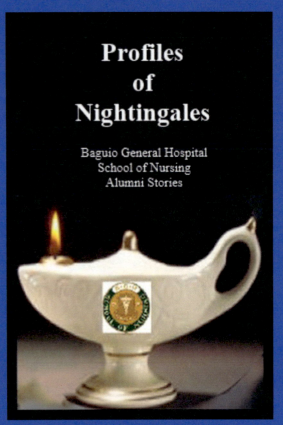

Inspired by the write-up on Crescencia 'Sising' Tamayo Vinluan, valedictory address of Eunice Bilagot Rios, touching attendance of Rosita Serdenia-Cabula to the reunion, articles on the Sharing a Grain and Shunt for Life, and overall mood generated by The Aftermath, suggestions are floating like "Why can't we write about the success stories of nurses," - specifically graduates of the Baguio General Hospital School of Nursing?

Swirling with this idea, we would like to know if there will be an interest among the BGHSNAA to want to be included in a compilation of success stories of BGH graduates during their career undertaking.

With a working title of Profiles of Nightingales - subtitled Baguio General Hospital School of Nursing Alumni Stories, we are contemplating that the Book will contain how the graduates progressed in their careers to include how their families thrived.

If there will be at least 50 who might want to be included in the profiles, we would go ahead with the project, identifying mechanics and costing.

If interested, please email the persons below. If we generate enough interest, we will get back to you and inform you of requirements.

Interest gathering will be up to February 28, 2025.

Nida Cristobal – nidasc123@yahoo.com
Fona Fornasdoro - trifona8484@gmail.com
Rudy D. Liporada - rodolfoliporada@gmail.com

What is your story?

Excerpts

Rudy D. Liporada
Director

rodolfoliporada@gmail.com
858-7221465

Rancho Costa Verde
Km. 52.5 Para Puertocitos
Baja, California

Each family story is colorful. Your future generations might want to know about those colors.

"He was the first from his Bontoc tribe to join the US Navy. There were no roads then from the hinterlands to Baguio. He crossed the mountains barefooted, garbed only with a 'ba-ag' loincloth." **-Memoirs of an Igorot-**

"Nonetheless, I always kid, saying, 'the only reason you joined the US Navy is to be able to come to America and marry me.'"
-Crescencia Vinluan, BGHSN Class 1953-

"We were so poor but I wanted to better myself, I went to Manila to study while working as a houseboy and security guard at the same time. I learned about how to join the US Navy…I left without telling anyone in my family…I just vanished…I came home during my first furlough…There were tears all over…" **-From the Memoirs of Primo-**

BFFs Instructors (l-r) Liway Luczon, Aurea Liporada, and Nida Cristobal

Liway: "The reunion was a singularly significant event I have attended. To witness how our graduates succeeded in their professions was so heartwarming to note - that our mentorship was part in producing well-qualified and well rounded individuals that we can now come together and enjoy, sharing our experiences and successes."

Aurea: "Rebonding with our former students was a memory lane of how they evolved from what they went through at the BGHSN to become - successful at their careers. The feeling of gratitude and pride was overwhelming to think that our mentorship was part of what shaped their successful chosen paths in life."

Nida: "Alumni reunions are events mentors and alumni should attend as they connect one to the past, present, and future. I feel joy and fulfillment whenever I think of my past with the BGHSN and extreme satisfaction seeing previous students and now colleagues who are successful in their nursing careers. Bottom line: As mentors, we did a good job."

"Sayang! We missed it!"

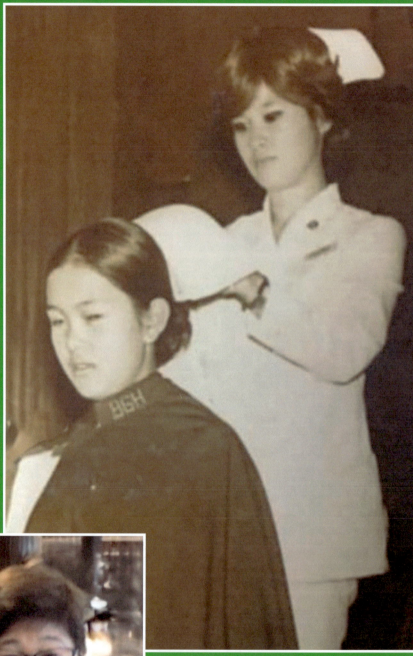

Mrs. Conchita 'Chit' Boquiren a former BGHSN Clinical Instructor and her husband, former army officer Albert Boquiren had earlier booked a cruise before the date of the 12th BGHSNAA International Grand Reunion was finalized. They could only sigh, "*Sayang! Nakaumay kami met kuma.*" Nonetheless, Chit was delighted to see the pictures of her former students and colleagues while perusing a sample copy of the ReminiscenceS along with her former co-instructors Nida Cristobal, Liway Luczon, and Aurea Liporada during their Christmas lunch at the Luczons in Dec. 19, 2024.

Chit is an RN graduate of the Ramon Magsaysay Memorial Medical Center. Before joining BGHSN, she was a private nurse at the Notre Dame Hospital while teaching at the Pines City Doctors Hospital. After her tenure at BGHSN, she moved on to the St. Louis University College of Nursing as assistant to the dean. There, she also obtained her Masters in Education, majoring in Educational Administration.

Immigrating to the US in 1983 with her husband and four children, she became a nursing professor, teaching Medical-Surgical and Maternity Nursing at the Citrus Community College. In 2002, she developed a Vocational Nursing curriculum for the Premier Career College where she bacame the first director. She retired in 2015.

Chit's husband is a graduate of the Officer Cadet School in Portsea, Australia. Assigned with the Philippine Army, his stints in the service included being with the Tactics Group of the PMA. He resigned his commission of 16 years to be with his family in the US.

Both now retired; and their children on their own, with one being a nun; they spend their time in leisure activities including traveling whenever and wherever they want.

It is in one of these travels, a cruise, that made them miss the BGHSNAAI Grand Reunion in Oct. 11-13, 2024.

So, "Sayang, we should have been there, too," they said. "So sorry we missed it."

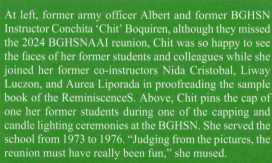

At left, former army officer Albert and former BGHSN Instructor Conchita 'Chit' Boquiren, although they missed the 2024 BGHSNAAI reunion, Chit was so happy to see the faces of her former students and colleagues while she joined her former co-instructors Nida Cristobal, Liway Luczon, and Aurea Liporada in proofreading the sample book of the ReminiscenceS. Above, Chit pins the cap of one her former students during one of the capping and candle lighting ceremonies at the BGHSN. She served the school from 1973 to 1976. "Judging from the pictures, the reunion must have really been fun," she mused.

Made in the USA
Columbia, SC
29 December 2024

525a81f5-3b79-4423-99fe-8d638eb97f8aR01